Revival Sermons

Revival Sermons

*

Notes of Addresses by
William C. Burns

*

Edited by M. F. Barbour

THE BANNER OF TRUTH TRUST

THE BANNER OF TRUTH TRUST
3 Murrayfield Road, Edinburgh EH12 6EL
PO Box 621, Carlisle, Pennsylvania 17013, USA

✳

First published 1869
First Banner of Truth Trust edition 1980
ISBN 0 85151 316 6

✳

Typeset, printed and bound in Great Britain by
Hazell Watson & Viney Ltd,
Aylesbury, Bucks

William Chalmers Burns, born in Dun, Scotland in 1815 died at the port of New Chwang, China in 1868. His life was characterised by a deeply-felt devotion to Jesus Christ wherever he was led. Licensed as a minister of the gospel in 1839 by the Church of Scotland, his anticipated departure to the East was delayed for several years while his remarkable gifts in evangelism were employed in Scotland and beyond. He was one of the group of young men God raised up in the days of M'Cheyne and the Bonar brothers whose only concern was for the universal triumph of the Cross. From the limelight of revival, he sailed to the obscurity of China in 1847, and laboured incessantly there, taking little rest, until on April 4 1868, he breathed his last words: 'Thine is the kingdom, the power, and the glory, for ever and ever.' In few lives have these words been more eloquently portrayed.

PREFACE

It is no longer the ocean that separates us from WILLIAM BURNS. His last utterance in the comfortless little inn of New-chwang, 'THINE IS THE KINGDOM, THE POWER, AND THE GLORY, FOR EVER AND EVER, AMEN,' he repeats now in heaven at his Master's feet.

During the twenty years which he spent in China, nothing was more eagerly greeted by the eyes of the few friends with whom he had time to correspond, than the sight, at considerable intervals, on the morning of mail day, of a letter from his hand. His consecration to the Master was so rare and so complete, during the years of his great work as an evangelist at home, that the sight of his handwriting reminded one to the last, that there are some who do illustrate the word, *Man's chief end is to glorify God*. The handwriting was unchanged by so many years' constant use of his adopted and much-loved hieroglyphic, and the signature of his last letters was exactly that which he used to affix in his youth to the tracts he gave to anxious inquirers, accompanied with the assurance of his interest and prayers.

In one of his letters he expressed gratitude for our having preserved and sought to circulate portions of his addresses.[1] He felt it to be 'supplying his lack of service'

[1] A former series of *Addresses by the Rev. William C. Burns, from a Hearer's Notes*, was published in 1859.

7

to his own countrymen. It is a privilege now, by publishing a few of these addresses in a collected form, to keep his words from falling to the ground. It was more his habit to study his *subject* beforehand than to compose his *sermon*, and his written style must not be judged by the notes of *extempore* speaking taken at the time without his knowledge. Yet these addresses, whatever they may have lost in their present form, are faithful memorials of days of awakening. Many will value them for their plain-spoken earnestness; and some will recognise in them the appeal of power—the arrow which the Lord sent home to bring them to the feet of Jesus.

Some of them are longer, because the speaker seemed compelled to press again and again on the vast audiences, assembled from great distances, the message of his Master. A few are short, having been compressed into the minutes which, in those days, working men could snatch, even during a snow-storm, from the breakfast-hour, to gather in the house of God around the open Bible. To how many a shop, or anvil, or clerk's desk, or attic, was then carried the manna portion, to be fed on there with joy, the Day will declare.

The reader will bear in mind, that such was the desire to hear the Word preached during the period when most of these addresses were delivered, that nine to twelve services were often held weekly. Extempore preaching alone could have adapted itself to embrace all the wants of the time.

The characteristics of the work of grace during the years 1839 to 1841, were thus noticed in an address from Mr

Burns's own pen, bearing the date September 1, 1841:

'Perhaps you have heard of the wonderful things which the great God has been doing for us in Scotland. The servants of Satan have reviled God's blessed work; and I wish to tell you something of the truth about it. You know that many people come from the church the same as they went to it; the Word does not touch their consciences, and they remain under the power of sin and Satan, of death and hell. This used to be very much the way among us until lately; but the God of love has visited us, and poured out his life-giving Spirit upon the dead souls of men. In some places you might see the solemn sight of hundreds weeping for their sins, and seeking to give up their hearts to Jesus. And, ah! what a sweet change has taken place on many! The high looks of the proud have been brought down; dead formalists have become living Christians; worshippers of Mammon have been changed into lovers of God; the blasphemous tongues of the profane have been made to sing God's praise; drunkards have cast from them the cup of devils, and have taken the cup of salvation; unclean persons, who used to be the slaves of lust, the drudges of the devil, the very dregs of humankind, are now sitting at the feet of Jesus; and some, who were ringleaders in every form of sin, are now bold and open, and unflinching in the service of Christ, even as once they were shameless, brazen-faced, and steel-hearted in the service of the Wicked One. Many, who formerly were dead in sin, are now living in the grace of Jesus, in the love of God, in the communion of the Spirit, and in the hope of heaven!'

At the present time, when many are stirred up to lay hold on the God of Pentecost, there is a special interest and pleasure in looking back to those days of his right hand—

days which, during succeeding times of deadness, it became almost saddening to recall.

The instruments then employed were ever made to feel that the entire power which accompanied the word resided in God the Holy Ghost, honoured as the living Jehovah, specially addressed in believing prayer, and shed forth in glorious power. Mr Burns was only in his twenty-fifth year in 1839–40, and did indeed ascribe all the glory of the effects of his preaching to God alone. The written Word was magnified. Sometimes inquirers would tell that what had been used to awaken them was the Scripture read or the psalm sung. The sanctuary was felt to be the very house of God. Reasons and excuses for absence, at other times insurmountable, how quickly they gave way! Daily labour was got over in time; and through the winter dark, or by the moonlight on the snow, eager hundreds were pressing to its gates, some still like burdened CHRISTIAN, others rejoicing in the Saviour newly found, and careless ones, who came from curiosity alone, had to sit and think, silent and still, for an hour in the crowd, till the service began. That solemn stillness was often followed by such requests for prayer as those which have become so common now—believers asking prayer for unconverted relatives, and awakened sinners asking it for themselves.

And when summer saw the services transferred to country and remote highland districts, like scenes were witnessed, like work was done. Not in churches, for these would have contained but a small portion of the listeners, but on the mountain side the gathered thousands worshipped. One ferryboat on one occasion had carried eight hundred hearers across the water by breakfast time. From a circuit of twenty miles they came. And the half-reaped harvest fields deserted on bright September afternoons, told that men and women, employers and employed, were intent on the momentous issues of that seed-time for eternity.

The world outside called it a passing excitement. Many within the church stood doubtingly aloof, noting all defects, and saying, 'Will it last?' Very faithfully were inquirers themselves warned, that everything about the work which had its rise in man only, must pass away, while all that was divine *must* last and outlive the grave, being sealed at death and confirmed at the judgment. The young among them were pointed to the fair blossom of 1840, covering the fruit trees, and told, that, if they were to come back in autumn and count the ripe apples, how few they would find in comparison with the blossom that cold winds had nipped and blown down. Or, away among the mountains,' Look at the young seedlings in the thick plantations, and say how many of them will stand in the forest in a hundred years' time.'

But the question, 'Did it last?' needs not to be repeated now. Deathbeds have answered it, lives have proved it, its fruits have been carried away and tested on many a distant shore; and district visitors have discovered, for hopeful converts fallen away, many more, who, unheard of in the day of revival, date impressions back to that time of blessing. A question nearer to the point might be, Does the God of the spirits of all flesh ever draw near to visit a congregation or a community without lasting fruits being produced, and without leaving each soul, who comes under the influence of it, or hears the report of it around, either awakened and quickened, or blighted and hardened? 'I will be as the dew unto Israel: his branches shall spread, and his beauty shall be as the olive tree and his smell as Lebanon.' 'They knew not that I healed them.' 'Master, behold the fig tree which thou cursedst is withered away' (*Hosea 14. 5–6; Mark 11. 21*.).

After 1847 Burns laboured among the Chinese, to whom he found free access, even in districts where treaty protection did not reach. Wearing their own costume, and possessed of several of their dialects, he was free to do the work of a pioneer. In some places God wondrously owned the labours of his servant; but in others he was made to feel how sovereign in his working is the life-giving Spirit, and how needful it was to call on believers for earnest and persevering prayer.

May it please the Master a second time to bless these comments on his own Word, and to stir up believers to remember before God the devoted missionaries who still in China stand face to face with an almost unbroken heathenism! May it not be humbly hoped that some who read this little volume, may be led to inquire how far they can aid in the work of that mission field, and by persevering, true prayer, hasten the day when the stone cut out without hands, the corner stone of Israel, shall smite the image of China's idolatry?

At a meeting of the China Mission, held in Edinburgh, the following tribute to Mr Burns was paid by the Rev. James Johnston, formerly his fellow-labourer in China:

'From the nature of the work for which he was specially qualified, and to which he entirely gave himself, that of a pioneer or evangelist—he could not expect to reap the fruits himself. His work was to break up the ground and sow the seed, not to gather the harvest. No man in this age, so far as we know, has so entirely devoted himself to this self-denying work.

'Again and again has our departed brother laboured for years in some dark and unpromising field, and just when the first streak of dawn appeared on the horizon, he would leave another to enjoy the glorious sun-rise, while he buried himself in some other region sunk in heathen darkness. Again and again have we seen him thus, in prayers and tears, sowing the precious seed, and as soon as he saw the green shoots appear above the dark soil, he would leave to others the arduous yet happy task of reaping the harvest, and begin his appointed work in breaking up the fallow ground. The full extent of his great life-work will not be known until that day, when "he soweth and he that reapeth shall rejoice together."

"The faith and patience of this devoted servant of God is an example to the church, and to every labourer in the Lord's vineyard, teaching us not to live upon the stimulus of a present success, even in the conversion of souls. No man enjoyed so great success as he did, or thirsted for the salvation of sinners with more intense longing than he, yet have we seen him labouring for seven years, according to his own testimony, without seeing one soul brought to Christ; yet labouring on only with increased diligence and prayer, until he saw, as he shortly did, the awakening at Peh-Chuia, which reminded him of Kilsyth. His influence in this way has been extended over a larger field; and with his strongly-marked individuality, he left the impress of his character and piety wherever he went. Missionaries felt it, and blessed God for even a casual acquaintance with William Burns; converts felt it, and have been heard to say, that they got their idea of what the Saviour was on earth, from the holy calm, and warm love, and earnest zeal of Mr Burns' walk with God. We bow to our Father's will in his removal on the 4th of April.

'His grave stands on the borders of the great kingdom of Manchuria, the advanced post of Christian conquests, beyond the northern limits of China, with the following inscription, in his own words:

To the Memory

OF THE

REV. WM. C. BURNS, A.M.,

MISSIONARY TO THE CHINESE

FROM THE

PRESBYTERIAN CHURCH IN ENGLAND.

BORN AT DUN, SCOTLAND, APRIL 1ST, 1815.

ARRIVED IN CHINA, NOVEMBER 1847.

DIED AT PORT OF NEW-CHWANG, APRIL 4TH, 1868.

II. Corinthians: V. Chap.

'The little mound casts its shadow over many lands, for where is Burns not loved and mourned? But his life is the church's legacy, and loudly calls to self-sacrifice and devotion to the cause of Christ, and especially the cause of missions. His indomitable spirit beckons us to the field of conflict and of victory, while his four last converts, the conquest of his death-bed, stand like sentinels by his grave, and long for the advance of the church's hosts.'

BONSKEID, PERTHSHIRE, *December 1868.*

CONTENTS

		PAGE
1.	PRESSING INTO THE KINGDOM *Luke 16. 16.*	19
2.	COVENANT MERCY *Isa. 54. 10.*	31
3.	THE LIMIT SET *Heb. 4. 7.*	41
4.	I AM DEBTOR *Rom. 1. 14*	57
5.	THE SECRET PLACE *Isa. 26. 20–21.*	69
6.	EVE OF THE DISRUPTION	84
7.	THE LORD PASSING BY *Ezek. 16. 6.*	91
8.	TRUE ZEAL *Gal. 4. 18.*	113
9.	UZZA SMITTEN *1 Chron. 13. 10.*	121
10.	RETURN OF THE ARK *1 Chron. 15.*	126
11.	TRIAL MADE SWEET *Rom. 12. 12.*	132
12.	THE BREAKER UP *Micah 2. 12–13.*	136
13.	WORDS OF WARNING *2 Thess. 2.*	144
14.	THE VALLEY OF VISION *Ezek. 37.*	155
15.	THE TEN VIRGINS *Matt. 25. 1–13.*	169
16.	SIN CONDEMNED *Rom. 8. 3.*	188
17.	A LETTER TO THE PEOPLE IN THE HIGHLANDS OF PERTHSHIRE	198

1

PRESSING INTO THE KINGDOM

[*Preached in St Leonard's Church, Perth, in the midst of the remarkable work of the Lord there, March 30, 1840.*]

'THE KINGDOM OF GOD IS PREACHED, AND EVERY MAN PRESSETH INTO IT.'—*Luke 16. 16.*

Without detaining you by noticing a number of things to which it would be necessary to allude, in order to shew the exact meaning of the expression, *Kingdom of God*, as considered with reference to what precedes or follows it in the passage, we shall consider the words of the text in their simple meaning.

First, What is meant by the kingdom of God? And second, What is meant by pressing into it? The kingdom of God is preached when Christ is preached, and then only. Wherever Jesus Christ is shewn to be the Son of God with power, to be an all-sufficient Saviour, a glorious Redeemer: wherever he is preached as Christ crucified, as Lord over all, as King: wherever his authority is supremely acknowledged, wherever he is adored as a Sovereign Ruler, his kingdom is preached, and men are invited to enter it.

When the kingdom of God is preached to *you*, you are invited to subject yourselves to Christ's authority, and to become faithful and devoted servants of Immanuel.

19

And now, what is meant by *pressing into* the kingdom? Let us seek to have a simple, but exact and spiritual view of this. Some persons find that their faith is darkened, and that difficulties are raised to their believing in Christ by the figures which are often employed. They say, 'I know I am to press into the kingdom, but what does this mean? I see no open door before me.' My dear friends, it simply means that, overcome by a sense of your own weakness, and feeling that you cannot have any hope of salvation from yourself, nor from any other, you throw yourself entirely on Christ's power, acknowledging yourself a willing subject of the King of kings.

You know what it is to press into any place where there is a great crowd; you do not stand listless at the door, you push your way, you press in and you enter. So it is with the kingdom of Christ; you see and feel that you must be in or you are lost, out for ever, banished to eternal darkness and torment, and therefore you press, you fight, till divine grace has subdued your proud spirit, and made you to enter into Christ's kingdom by Christ, the way, the truth, the life.

We shall now mention one or two things which ever distinguish this pressing into the kingdom. First, there is *a supreme desire* to enter. The Christian has many pursuits in which he must engage; but when a man begins to feel the necessity of being in the kingdom, these at once take a subordinate place, and become of very second-rate importance. His choice is to be saved, to enter, to belong to Christ.

Many make this a desire among other desires. They say, 'Well, we wish to be saved, we wish to get an interest in Christ;' but then that is not their *only* wish. They wish to be rich and great, to be esteemed and honoured, and—they wish to have Christ too. Dear friends, that will not do. No, if you wish to have all these things, and after them to have Christ, or if you wish to have Christ just in the same proportion, or even if you wish to have Christ as a first object, but *must* have these other things along with him, Christ will never be yours. You must either desire to have Christ before all, above all, alone, or you must be contented to do without him altogether. Now, I am sure there are some of you, who, if you could get a half Christ, Christ's merits, and a few of your own merits along with them; if Christ would but take a middle place, would consent to reign with other kings, to divide the government with Satan, with riches, with man's good opinion, or even with your own, *you would have him*, and gladly give him a second, or even an equal place in your heart with the world and vanity. Christ will not consent to this. He must be *all* or *nothing*: king, sovereign, ruler, governor, or absent altogether. Now, what is he to you? Is he on the throne? or only on the footstool? This is a question which may shew you whether you are really pressing in.

Would you be contented to give up all for Christ, and take him alone? If possessing him were to deprive you of all you have, and all you hope for, would you bid adieu to that *all*—and to the Christian it is a *little* all—and say, 'Come, Lord Jesus, thine be the kingdom?'; if not, it is because you know nothing of Christ, his character, his person, or his love. He is nothing to you. The believer, who has begun to learn the value of Christ, does not find difficulty in determining whether to give up one thing, or two things, or many things for Christ, and whether he should still be repaid for so doing. He is not always hesitating and calculating whether Christ will make up this or that loss to him. He has Christ, thrice blessed portion, and in him, all. He would not seek earthly riches or honours, even if he could get them. All he has, all he is, is already Christ's—by purchase—by free surrender—and by wonderful, glorious exchange. All that Christ has is his too, he is a joint-heir with Christ. He gets all *from* heaven, returns all to heaven, and the heart that is already at home there has not much time for earthly pleasure.

We do not mean to say that the Christian refuses this world's comforts or enjoyments when they come in his way. They, too, are sweet, and why? Because they are a proof of Christ's goodness, love, and tender care. But we do say that the believer will not be very anxious or careful about them; nor will he have either pleasures or profits which Christ does not give him. He will not receive gains in a business unlawful, or in ways disapproved by the Lord. He asks for nothing, but *what the Lord wills:* can enjoy nothing, but what he can enjoy in Christ, because without Christ it were no enjoyment to him. Does he receive any temporal gift—an estate for instance—he does not rashly give it up, he takes it back to Christ, and says, Thou hast sent this, Lord, what wilt thou have me to do with it?

The difference between his unconverted and converted state lies here. Before, he considered himself master of all he possessed. 'I have earned this; I have laboured for it, I have got it, and *it is mine*, for my gratification, my amusement, my use.' But now, he is changed from a master into a servant, he looks on himself merely as a steward, who has received so much, whether it be a fortune, time, or talents, from Christ, to be used for his glory; and his only wish is to be a faithful, prudent steward, serving Christ in all things. 'Whom have I in heaven but thee? and there is none upon earth that I desire beside thee'.

And now, no false friends, no open enemy, neither a lying devil, nor a hostile world, neither terror without, nor treachery within, shall be able to take Christ out of your heart, nor to prevent your entrance into the celestial city.

Choose him alone. This is what Enoch did, what David did, for he desired none in heaven but the Lord; what Peter did, for he said, Lord, to whom shall we go?—what every saint is joyfully constrained by his love to do! Some would take Christ if they might even be allowed to choose the time when he should be their all, if they might do it in the church or in private, but not in the world. But if you are his, you will choose Christ to-night, Christ to-morrow, Christ for ever; Christ in the private room, and in the family; Christ in the shop, and in the market; Christ in the church and in the world; Christ when you are with the godly; Christ when with the ungodly and profane; Christ in the hour of prosperity, Christ in the hour of adversity; Christ when the world smiles, and says, as it sometimes seems to do, that *Christ is good*; and Christ when the world frowns, and says that Christians are mad, and that Christ has a devil. You will take Christ with you to the humble cottage and to the lordly mansion; Christ among your poor and despised fellow-sinners; Christ with the nobles of the land; Christ in the drawing-room—I do not say Christ in the ball-room, for if you go there, you must leave Christ behind; I do not say Christ in the theatre, for you must get Satan to go with you there; but Christ in life, Christ in death, Christ in the day of judgment, and then— ineffably glorious hope—Christ to all eternity.

We have tried to shew you that to have Jesus for one's

portion is the believer's ruling desire. Secondly, *a firm resolution* is necessary to the attainment of this, as well as of every other great object. When a crowd is rushing into this church, for instance, and you stand aloof, and make no exertion, you must remain outside. But you try to be first, you force your way, you succeed, and secure a place. If you would enter by the golden gate of mercy, you must resolve to enter, and not to be disappointed. Some say, 'I wish to get in, but I need not go to the entrance, it is closed up, there is one barrier, there is another impassable.' Now, such a wavering, doubting soul as that will never enter: *that* is not pressing into the kingdom. No obstacle must terrify you, or drive you back. They are not of *his creating* whose it is to open, and no man is able to shut. Submit to Jehovah Jesus. Will he disappoint you? No, he will direct your way, support, strengthen, comfort you. He will guide you through the narrow straits of repentance into the open sea of faith, with its wide-spread views, its gilded distance, its boundless prospects. Nor *there* will he leave you, but traversing its waters along with you, and pointing your course to yonder brilliant coast, he will at last bring your little bark into the haven of eternal rest.

Young believer! that sea is not always smooth; the sky overcasts, and though your course may be for a time through the still cool waters, difficulties will come at last. There are sacrifices to be made, trials to be suffered—sometimes agonies to be endured, for if thy hand offend thee cut it off; it is better for thee to enter into life maimed, than having two hands to go into hell: where their worm dieth not, and the fire is not quenched. If thy right hand cause to offend, it must be sacrificed, great as the sacrifice may be. Here the religion of many is over, they never get as far as this. Many would take Christ if they might have him without his cross. Some one says, 'I would accept of Christ, but my business is not a lawful one, so I cannot come;' that man's business is the right hand which he ought to cut off, but will not. Another says, 'I would press into the kingdom, but if I were to become a Christian, I should lose all my employment and my customers.' 'If I were to begin to be religious, I should become bankrupt,' as a man said once to me. No man ever became bankrupt by believing in Christ. Such as these have a right hand, a right foot, that they cannot sacrifice. Another says, 'I have married a wife, she will not come with me, and I will not go without her.' And how many a wife says, 'I would go, but my husband will not; I must wait for him!'

You see, then, that *all* is to be surrendered for Christ. If any of you who are servants find it impossible to serve God in the situation you occupy, you should even leave your places to follow him. Specially, any business that is un-lawful, or where your gains are got by doubtful means, is to be given up—forsaken; and the dearer such a *right hand*—such an idol—may be to you, the more certainly necessary is it to cut it off. There are some who go a considerable length in this, and yet fall short. They will part with the left hand, but 'we *cannot* spare the right,' they say. And so you are to be contented with the loss of Christ, to keep a right hand, a right foot. Oh! what madness. We don't *deny* that the process is painful—agonising sometimes. Those who have never had to suffer it can scarce be Christians. Who will say it is not painful to give up a darling lust? to lay down at Immanuel's cross a long-cherished idol, which has insensibly remained, perhaps when we thought that all our idols had been cut off and died at his feet? To give up the loved society of one who has been ever dear and affectionate, and has stood by us in distress—to give up the favourite companion of early youth, or the friend of riper years, because that companion and that friend refuse to be the friends of Jesus! Trials like these, and there are trials harder still, must be borne, if we would follow Christ.

To break off with a rude shock from a vicious habit strengthened by years of continuance, to crush a passion which has come to rule us with an iron hand, to be roused by such a sense of coming vengeance amid our follies and our crimes as tears us from our tyrant's grasp—feeling that Christ can never come to rule in the same bosom—then to begin to oppose them, to check them, struggle with them, grapple for the mastery—trials like these are fearful to flesh and blood. Flesh and blood *alone* never bore them. There we feel our weakness, and there it is that we learn to take *all* our strength from the arm on which we lean; encouraged by his promise, 'My grace is sufficient for thee.'

And those only who have made the proof, have the least idea of the consolations imparted by Christ to his obedient followers. The bitter sacrifice yields the peaceable fruits of righteousness. Sweet, *sweet*, SWEET to make a sacrifice for Jesus! High, pure, lasting enjoyment flows in. The bitterness soon goes, and nothing remains but a sense of his love, and the peace passing all understanding, that is attendant on one smile from Immanuel. Never, never did one of his beloved saints, whom he has purchased with his own blood, undergo the pain of amputating a limb for him, without also experiencing the abundance of his consolations, and the fulness of his love. The limb is off, the pain will soon be gone; the strength is exhausted by the wound, but Immanuel comes with the oil of consolation in his hand; he applies the balm of his own eternal love to the afflicted soul, raising it up once more, and putting a new song into its mourning lips, even thanksgiving to our God.

Has he been thus coming near to any of *you?* Who has been cutting off offending members? Who has been exclaiming with Ephraim, 'What have I to do any more with idols?' I know some present have, within the last few weeks, or even days; and was it not a hard struggle, was it not severe? It was severe. But, dear brothers and sisters in Jesus, are you still weeping, are the consolations of God small with you? No, no! But keep steadfast, keep steadfast, the battle may be nearer than you think; you are not yet in your Father's house; Satan is in that bosom still, he once reigned there; Jesus holds his place now; but though unseated, his malice and his rage burn yet the more, and, though a dying, he is not an inactive foe. He will be all the more anxious to distress and torment you because his time with you is short, and because he has lost you as his prey. The world, though now it seems to have lost its hold, though it no longer entrances you, though you are no more its slave, the world is what it was before, and all too soon will it intrude into the bosom that is now insensible to its charm and tinsel pleasure.

The flesh is not yet dead, though it is crucified. It struggles, and will struggle on till death is swallowed up of life. The evil heart of unbelief, which so long kept you from Jesus, and the passions which have been calmed for a while, will rise again.

Return now to the last part of the figure employed in the text by which we have been illustrating our subject. The plucking out of a right eye implies that even the most tender and delicate parts of our being are to be sacrificed. The eye being the beauty of the countenance and the most precious part of the body, its loss disfigures and deforms; and even among inconsiderate and wicked companions, exposes to derision and contempt. The agony, too, attendant on the extraction of an eye, has perhaps more of torture in it than anything that can be suffered; and yet this expression is not thought too strong. Even those *cruel mockings* which are so much dreaded, are to be patiently endured, and even gloried in, for the reproach of Christ is better than all the treasures of Egypt.

Here is another distinguishing mark of the true believer. He alone receives courage to quit himself like a man, and to be strong in the Lord. There are fair weather Christians, who are godly among the godly, but whose devotion disappears when they enter a profane or worldly circle. They set out fair for heaven, as they and others think, but the first time the sky lowers, and the black cloud appears, they recoil from the dangers of the passage and draw back. At a time of wide-spread blessing, especially, there are many such; they present a fair outside, and a deceiving attention to the things of heaven. Friends and relations are setting out for heaven, the day is fine, the sea is calm, the sky cloudless—they go on board the vessel that is leaving for a distant shore; they admire it, and think they would almost like to go too; but no sooner is the vessel in motion, than they cry, 'Put me on shore, put me on shore.' They are landsmen, and they get afraid. Miserable turncoats, two-faced hypocrites, men that hoist different flags, sailing under English colours when they come near an English man-of-war, and raising another flag when the enemy comes in sight. They have a godly face and a profane face, just as it happens to suit; they assume the one whenever they are with Christians, and talk of sermons and ministers, nay, sometimes talk of Christ; but as soon as the scene changes, they have a suitable face for the ungodly, and join in the jeer and the laugh, mocking and scoffing just as others do. How different do some appear to their minister when they meet him, compared with what they are in the family or the workshop.

As I was conversing with a stranger one day on the subject of religion, he spoke with much apparent feeling about very serious and interesting things. That man is surely a Christian, I thought; he fears God. Soon after I met him in a shop where he was well known, and where he was transacting business. He immediately spoke to me as he had formerly done. When he left the shop, the master of it said to me, 'Is *that* man serious?' I merely answered, '*You* should know.' 'I could not have thought it; he seemed till now to be as careless as others, and not more particular about honest dealing, but ready to take an advantage where he might.'

At this very point you will discover a true believer. He does not change his colours. He is the soldier of Christ everywhere. He carries his high character with him, and sustains it all through. When circumstances oblige him to mix with the unconverted devotees to this world's pleasure, his bearing is the same or even more marked than when among his fellow-Christians. A light word kindles his indignation though he be silent. If the reproach be on the name of his ever dear and glorious Redeemer, he takes no part, he is like an individual unelectrified in a room where all the rest of the party are so. He hasn't got hold of the chain. The scoffing or ill-natured hit stops at him; he does not catch the smile that flies round the circle when the name of saint is mentioned with a sneer. All his wish is to be a saint. It matters not to him what men say or think, if only he be doing, from love to Jesus, what he believes Jesus would command him to do, so that none can be long near him without perceiving the despised mark of the Lamb. You may sometimes read on his very brow the stamp which the seal of the Spirit has impressed there. Whether does he pray more, think you, when he is going to visit at a house where Christ is honoured, or when he must go to one where the fashionable votaries of this world dwell? Ah! it will be the latter. He will not try how far he can alter his style among them; his look will speak when his word cannot, for he is tender of his Saviour's honour among unbelieving men. He watches for an opportunity to bear witness to Jesus; he would rather bear all the mocking that a world could heap on him than let a breath of contempt fall upon his Lord, remembering that him will the King of kings confess before his Father and the hosts of heaven.

Dear fellow-believer, you who have lately come to know him, the tempter will assail you, in an unguarded hour he will be upon you, and you will deny Christ almost before you are aware, if you do not make up your mind to pluck out this right eye, and so to press into the kingdom.

2

COVENANT MERCY

[April 6th, 1840, a Farewell Address given in St Leonard's Church, to the converts gathered in during the Revival in Perth, after three months' labour there, on his leaving for Aberdeen.]

'FOR THE MOUNTAINS SHALL DEPART, AND THE HILLS BE REMOVED; BUT MY KINDNESS SHALL NOT DEPART FROM THEE, NEITHER SHALL THE COVENANT OF MY PEACE BE REMOVED, SAITH THE LORD THAT HATH MERCY ON THEE.'—*Isaiah 54. 10.*

This promise is threefold. God has given to his church love and peace. These blessings come to the saints through God's covenant. These blessings and that covenant are everlasting. Jehovah confers on his people mercy, peace, and kindness. He shews mercy, free, sovereign, unconditional, not connected in any degree with what he finds in the sinner, but flowing from God alone, this being his prerogative, peculiar to himself. He shews mercy; the Lord is merciful and gracious. How much is contained in that golden sound, Mercy, mercy!

Believer, what does it bring to your mind to hear of mercy? Ah! it is sweet when you are weighed down with a sense of guilt and sin—when you see yourself all but lost, to hear of mercy. You feel how deeply you need it, that if there were no mercy with Jehovah, you must perish. You found out your need of mercy when first you saw your sin to be transgression against an infinitely holy God. When the sinner begins to learn something of what Jehovah is, somewhat of the perfections of his glorious nature and character, he is overwhelmed, he cannot conceive any possibility of salvation, so great is the distance separating the holy Creator from an offending and unholy creature.

If in this world we were, but for an instant, to see sin as God sees it, we should die, the sight would drink up our spirits; but this is not permitted, sin is not yet unveiled to the eye of the believer, his capacities are not made to sustain the revelation of the glory of God. He sees mercy now, but in a dim light. Ah! but in heaven, *how* glorious, how amazing, how overpowering! It will be the anthem of the redeemed, 'There is mercy with God.' New harps they will need for this song, ever new. You know little of sin, you that have seen it most. You have seen but the smallest part of it, but God sees it all, and looks at it with an infinitely holy eye, from the least to the greatest of it. It seems wonderful to you to have pardoning mercy extended to your heinous sins, and the least of them looks heinous beheld by the light of God's word. Ah! what will you think of mercy when you reach the blessed shore of heaven!

Unbeliever! your eye rests on the sin you committed last. It looks blackest. But God sees each offence, since ever you began to sin, in its full enormity; his eye sees no difference, time does not change guilt in his sight. The sin of last year is as vivid as the one you are now committing. Old man! the sins of sixty years are all as vividly before God as those of twenty, and every one of them seems to him more black than any sin was ever seen to be by man. You are a vile object in his sight. One sin, and another, and another, on to millions, with their aggravations, rise in the dark catalogue of crime in God's reckoning book against you. Believer, such a catalogue once stood there against you, but there was mercy with God. On that word your hopes are built. Do you not see the glorious sovereignty of his mercy; full, because blotting out all sin, even the greatest; free, because unmerited, unpurchased, unconditional, and offered to all.

It is sad to hear how some of God's people speak of mercy. From the way in which God is generally pleased to bring them to himself, they seem to think that their convictions and repentance must come first, and then afterwards the pardon of God through Christ is given, thus putting their tears and humiliation as almost a condition appointed by God.

This will never give you an exalted idea of the sovereignty of God's mercy in Christ; oh never! Dear believers, brethren in Christ, forget yourselves altogether: look beyond yourselves. Look back as far as you can into eternity, and hear Jehovah by an act of grace proclaiming your pardon, choosing you, in spite of everything in yourself, as an object of mercy. He waited not to pardon you, till he saw you beginning to melt at the thought of his love, or to repent at the thought of your sins. He pardons like a God. He loved you while you were still in your sins, and set his heart to deliver you. He loves you now, and he will deliver you. He loved you long before the foundations of the world were laid, and he will love you on. Had it depended in the slightest degree on you, where had you been now? Not saved! He loved us just because he loved us. He shewed us mercy because he will have mercy.

There are different ways of shewing mercy. You may do it in a kind way, or you may do it as a tyrant would to a slave. Now, the Lord's lovingkindness is

33

gloriously manifested in his mercy. His children do not always trust him for this: they ofttimes dishonour him by accounting him a hard Master and not a tender Father. Some of you suffered much at the beginning of your course from the fear of condemnation and conviction of sin. You judged the Lord's dealings as harsh and cruel, and you said, 'Surely his purposes towards me are not good, he cannot love me, or I should not suffer thus.' But what are you thinking of his dealings now, when you are lifted out of the miry clay and standing on the rock? Are you not singing, 'He hath done all things well?' and now you would not wish to have been without any of the suffering you had to endure. He has brought you by a way that you knew not, just that he might reveal to you the more brightly the purposes of his love.

The paths through which we are led seem often crooked and rough and dark while we are in them, but when we have come through them, they all look straight, and the path will yet be seen to have been the shortest and safest and easiest that we could have taken. So shall it appear when we reach heaven. There are many dark providences in the course of God's dealings with his people, which they will never understand in this lower world, but which shall yet draw from them the eternal hallelujah; every one of them will then lie unfolded to the eye, replete with loving-kindness.

The beautiful figure in the beginning of our text makes all explanations regarding the stability of the covenant unnecessary. Since the flood, these hills have not changed. Immutable, they stood looking down on our fathers' graves, as they soon will look down on ours, seeming to mock at man and his concerns, and to tower over his little-ness. But these very mountains will pass away, while the elements are melting with fervent heat. Your souls, believers, will then be entering into the joy of your Lord, standing secure at Immanuel's side in the kingdom which cannot be moved. The mountains shall depart, but the covenant of peace shall not remove. It remains immoveable from the nature of the contracting parties. It was formed between the Father and Jesus the Prince of Peace, whose goings are from everlasting. Doubting believers! you would not be so full of fears if you would think more of this. You vacillate, and change, and waver. The covenant has nothing to do with *you*, you are not one of the contracting parties. All you have to do is to become interested in it, by believing that Immanuel has satisfied divine justice and reconciled you to God, and then at once to rejoice in the well-ordered covenant.

See what confirms the covenant. It is the authority of God. It is Jehovah's seal. It is, 'Thus saith the Lord, that hath mercy on thee.' Is he man that he should lie? How often, believer, do you think of the Lord as if he were one like yourself? you suppose that when *you* change Eternal Love fluctuates. Look back and see him loving you in a past eternity, for no reason but that he set his heart upon you. Look forward and see him receiving you into glory. Not even sin can change his love to you. Will a believer sin because grace abounds? When a man comes within an approach to that, it only shews that he has nothing to do with the covenant. But you, believers, who would rather die than pierce Immanuel afresh by sin, to you we say, that the sin you have committed never can have changed the nature of an everlasting covenant: you can never fall away from the covenant if once you have an interest in it. You may fall *in* the covenant (and in a way to destroy your present peace, and bring down Jehovah's chastening hand), but you never can fall *out* of the covenant.

If sin grieves you, if you forsake it, his kindness shall yet return to you, the covenant of his peace shall not be removed saith the Lord, who hath mercy on thee. Mercy was needed to predestinate you; mercy to elect and call you; mercy to justify you; mercy to begin the glorious work of sanctification in your soul; and mercy shall open the golden gate of glory. Mercy pardoned your first offence; but for mercy the least of them would have sunk you into hell; and no more than mercy was required to pardon the blackest ever committed by man. How can you lose a part in a covenant whose very pledge and bond is mercy? There is no room in it for a repenting sinner's perdition. Mercy never condemned a man when justice had been satisfied. That no doubts may remain, and as if to prevent the very possibility of fear, it is the LORD who hath mercy, that sends the message to you.

Believer, when you try to live as in sight of that great white throne, you will rejoice. Why live so far below your privileges as to be cast down or distressed at anything that can befall you here? Anticipate heaven! Look forward, forward. Get on a very few years by faith, bound over them, and you are beyond this sphere of mortality, and earth has passed away. Rise far, far above mist and shadow, cloud and darkness, and get into the ethereal blue sky of God's eternal love. Won't that make you holy? Ah! no man that lives much in heaven, can look on sin without abhorrence.

In parting with you, we have no farewell to say but this: Come to Christ now. Let him reign over you. And you, dear lambs of the flock, keep close to Christ. Ah! you were never so happy before; continue, then, ever where you now are, sitting at the feet of Jesus. We shall meet at the great white throne; till then you need none other arm around you but Christ's to keep you from falling. You have Christ, you have heaven. Blessed portion of the saints! Thrice happy are you; in due time you shall rise to glory, and so shall you be ever with the Lord.

As his redeemed, you will have a high place there. Angels have but the angels' place. Glorious they are, and they excel in strength; but you will be nearer the throne than cherubim or seraphim, for you are joint-heirs with Christ. What a glorious destiny is yours! To his angels he has given their places, their offices, their beauty, their glory, and they serve him day and night. To you he has given his Son—even the Only-begotten, the unspeakable gift. It is one of the most glorious of his titles now, that he is *Saviour*; and angels have got a new song unconceived of even in heaven till Jesus died, 'Worthy is the Lamb that was slain,' and they hymn the anthem with a wonder ever new. Look up, and sing with the countless multitude. Their names were once as unworthy and as vile as yours, but they were written from all eternity in blood, in the Lamb's book of life. Will it not be heaven to be with Jesus, who washed your sin away in his own blood? to bask in the golden rays of a sun that has even now risen upon you?

Might we but hope that we should all meet on the right hand! We shall not all be there. Such a thing never happened yet. Who in this vast assemblage consents to that awful thought? Who is saying, '*I* shall not be there, I shall be on the left hand?' Can it be? 'I am determined to go to hell.' Not in words, but practically, has it been said by many in this city, who have openly opposed this work of God. Many have mocked it; some now present have mocked at it all along; some here have, perhaps, come to mock again. Will you mock at the day of judgment? Will you mock the Judge? Dear friends, they do not mock in hell. And you mistake much if you think you can hurt God's servants by mocking them, or retard God's work, or keep one penitent out of heaven. The everlasting arm is round each trembling believer; you hurt no one but yourself, and you will feel this bitterly to all eternity.

Some members have been taken out of *your* family, and you are left. You, man, have to say, I am yet a drunkard. You, I am dishonest still. You, I am a Sabbath breaker still. You, I am a swearer still. You, I still am unclean; I have been warned, I have been entreated, I have held out against everything; I am unchanged, I am filthy still.

It will be sad from hell to look back to nights like these, when so many were converted savingly around you, and came under the power of the Spirit of our God. It will be sad to remember how near Jesus came, and how you all but touched him in the passing by—to remember that it was there and then that you refused his love. To you, dear fellow-sinners, we say no more. We have sought to present to you a law condemning, a God incensed, justice provoked, hell opened, Jesus a Saviour—and he is waiting now.

Many there are whom we cannot reach: who put themselves at a distance from the Word, and seek to encase themselves in worldliness. There are the proud, the rich, the great; there are ladies and gentlemen that will not be awakened till judgment, impervious to the darts of terror, deaf to the sweet calls of Immanuel's love. How sad it will be for you, my friends, to find out that your name has been omitted from the Book of Life! Many a viler name than yours will be found in it. There are many now in hell who have not committed half the sins that some now in heaven did. Many a larger and blacker account than yours you will see blotted out with blood. Many whom you have despised as criminals, as profane, you will see passing into glory when you are going away to make your bed in hell.

I was struck to-night on coming here, to find the multitude standing outside the locked gates, because the church was full, and as they stood, some wept that they could not enter the sanctuary. I thought of the awful sentence to be pronounced when the door is shut; and I told them they had got a better sermon to-night than they could have got in church. 'Take Christ away with you; the heavenly temple is not yet full.'

In parting, dear young believer, remember these lines—

> *Satan trembles when he sees*
> *The weakest saint upon his knees.*

He is never more disappointed than when his temptations drive men to Christ. He, then, is the means of driving a soul to its fortress, its security. Prayer is strength. No Christian can thrive without being much alone with God. None who are so can do otherwise than thrive. Fight by prayer when you are fainting. As to your companionships, try to be most where you will be nearest to Jesus. Young Christian, be much in your secret place, and He cannot forsake you. Pray for us! Pray for your minister. Some people seem to think it is casting a slur on their minister when they are told to pray for him. No godly minister will despise his people's prayers. It was a slur that was cast on Paul; and the minister who is too proud to ask the prayers of the saints is too proud to be honoured in the conversion of souls.

Conclude by singing these verses—

Our souls, we know, when He appears,
Will bear His image bright,
And all His glories full disclosed
Shall open to our sight.

A hope so great and so divine,
May trials well endure,
And purge the soul from sense and sin,
As Christ himself is pure.

3

THE LIMIT SET

[*The sermon, of which the following are but fragments, was preached while Burns was a guest at Bonskeid, in the church of Tenandry, which is situated in the birch wood overhanging the Pass of Killiecrankie, on Wednesday evening, September 9, 1840. This service lasted from five o'clock till nine, beginning early for the convenience of those who had long distances to walk home; and continued late because the hearers hung upon the preacher's words until the sun had set and the full moon had arisen. It was a memorable night in the history of many.*]

'AGAIN, HE LIMITETH A CERTAIN DAY, SAYING IN DAVID, "TO-DAY," AFTER SO LONG A TIME; AS IT IS SAID, "TO-DAY IF YE WILL HEAR HIS VOICE, HARDEN NOT YOUR HEARTS".'—*Hebrews 4. 7.*

The words here quoted are, as we see from the text itself, from the book of Psalms. They form part of an exhortation to the church in Israel from Jehovah, the Head of the church, warning them from the fate of their unbelieving and rebellious forefathers, not to abuse his long-suffering, nor to presume upon his grace by hardening their hearts through the deceitful nature and soul-blinding influence of sin.

An offer of mercy had been made to Israel. All the day Jehovah had stretched out his hands to a disobedient and gainsaying people, who had, through unbelief, refused to enter in, having not only killed the prophets and stoned them which were sent unto them, but crucified the Holy and the Just One. And, my dear friends, having persisted in this, they were given over to a reprobate mind, God swearing in his wrath that they should not enter into his rest. Ah! it is a fearful thing when God gives a man over; when, while yet the short day of life in this world lasts, the day of grace has fled for ever; when the long-suffering Immanuel ceases to knock at the door of the heart; when the last striving of his Spirit is over.

My friends, your day of grace has lasted long; many are the offers of pardon and reconciliation, many the declarations of grace and mercy, many the proclamations of forgiveness and of peace that have been repeated in your ears again and again. They have come by ministers, by religious friends, by conscience, ay, and by the very Spirit of Jehovah himself, in the hearing of your outward ear, and in the hearing of your inward heart; and yet, through unbelief, are you sitting here this very evening in your natural state, dead, unpardoned, impenitent, unchanged; exposed to the thunders of vengeance, without a covert.

'Again, he limiteth a certain day.' The idea which these words convey is inexpressibly sweet and comforting in one sense, though truly awful in another. We may just suppose a case. A man is going fast along a road—a rebel and disobedient. His master says to him, 'If you *stop* and *turn*, before you come to such and such a point, I *will* forgive you.' Yet the man refuses, persists, and runs madly on. The kind master, unwilling to see his servant ruined, in his love, as it were, extends the point of turning, stretches the limit, and places the boundary line of life further on.

So it is, beloved friends, with your God. A thousand

times has he removed the line which finally excludes from his mercy; every sermon he has extended it; every Sabbath has seen it still distant. And this night again he limits a certain day—a day of mercy and pardon, a day of love and grace. But this day may be the last. His long-suffering does know a limitation and an end. It may be that God is saying of you, impenitent sinner, that if to-day you turn not, he shall swear in his wrath you shall never, never enter into his rest. 'To-day, after so long a time.' Ah! sinner, can you stand that? Listen how he pleads with you, *after so long a time*. You know it has been long; long has he waited, pleaded, and besought you, and yet you are keeping him at the door of your heart.

'To-day if ye *will* hear his voice.' The word *will* should be more correctly rendered *shall*, expressing merely the possibility or event of hearing God's voice, and not, as is often thought, the inclination or willingness to hear it. For instance, thousands never hear God's voice. These words are therefore used in the sense of, *If* ye shall hear, If ye shall be *permitted* to hear his voice. And, in a sense, these words may be addressed to all of you. Ah! there are many here who have never yet heard God's voice. Thousands are dying daily who, though a preached gospel has rung in their ears from the cradle to the grave, have never heard in their hearts a single word of God. There is nothing which man is naturally so unwilling to listen to as the words of God. He will listen with avidity to anything else; he will listen to his friends, listen to tales about his neighbours, listen to evil, and listen to good. Yes, he will come to the church and listen to the minister—few are unwilling to do that; he will come to the courts of Jehovah, saying, 'I must go and hear a sermon; I wonder what the minister will say to us to-day.' And so long as the minister tells him something new, so long as he goes on fluently, the man will be quite pleased, and even, perhaps, talk with his family about how the minister pleased him, and what the minister said. Ay, but notice the difference when the minister happens to rehearse in a people's hearing the words of Jehovah HIMSELF, the reading of *his* word is listened to with a sleepy carelessness that shews the man regards it not; and then, if the minister happens to quote a passage from that Word of God, ah! you may see by the man's expression that it's a sort of interruption to the thread of the discourse, an uninteresting, though, perhaps, necessary intrusion of what is merely used to shew that a fact is correct or a doctrine true. Friends, don't your consciences tell you that what we are saying is true? Don't deny it. You know you feel it; and yet, what madness is this!

Suppose that one of the inmates of the palace of our Queen were observed paying particular attention whenever any of the attendants or household spoke, but whenever the Queen spoke, seemed inattentive and wishing the interruption were over—such a thing was never heard of; and yet, Sabbath after Sabbath, and year after year, do you come into the house of God, and listen to his servants, but the Master of the house you will not hear. You will listen to the words of any of his creatures, but when Jehovah speaks, it's not worth your while to pay the deference you do to a fellow-mortal. His voice may be heard by you to-night; the ears of the deafest sinner in this house may be unstopped, if he will not persist in hardening his heart against the strivings of the Spirit.

'If ye will hear his voice, harden not your hearts.' The heart of man is hard as stone. It cannot be softened by any natural process. It never can be melted. It is possible, so to speak, to break it in pieces, just as by violence you may break any hard substance; but, ah! it won't melt, it won't bend, it won't yield but to the fire of the love of the gospel. The mere outward hearing of the word won't do it. It may seem to have an effect, but the man does not hear the word as the voice of God. The heart is like the hard anvil; when struck by the hammer there is a great sound made, and some sparks are emitted, but the anvil is hard still. But still, my dear friends, hard as our hearts by nature are, it is possible to make them harder still. *Harden not your hearts.* True, we received them at the first hard as adamant as to any capability of loving God, and their nature is unchangeable but by the power which creates us anew in Christ Jesus; but then there is a second hardening of the heart already hard. There are various means which tend to this: as,

First, *Indifferent hearing.* We have already spoken of this, but it is so important, that we would seek to impress it still more upon you. It is an awful thing to shut the ear against the voice of God. You do not know how few may be your opportunities. There may be some before me to whom *this* is the limited period, whose day of hope is quickly sinking down to the night of despair; but to whom Jehovah is still, though for the last time, saying, *Harden not your hearts.* How do you know, sinner, that he is not saying that to you, and yet, there you are as thoughtless and as unconcerned—as deaf as ever. It is awful when a soul thus begins to harden under the repeated strivings of the Spirit, and the gracious calls of the gospel. Some of you here are in that state. Fellow-sinner, don't harden your heart against another call. You say, 'It is hard already.' I believe it well; yes, hard as these rocks under your feet, but don't let it get harder still. Poor sinner, you remember the day when it was not quite so hard, when it could shrink from sin, when you thought it could even melt at the love of Immanuel? Ah! you say, 'I remember when it was not so icy cold, and insensible as it is now. I remember when a father's frown could move me, when a mother's tears could make me weep, and when a mother's prayers could touch my heart. I remember when the sermons which I heard used to impress me and fill me with alarm and sorrow; but now, the minister may say what he likes, it's all one, you'll never make me feel now— nothing, nothing can soften a hardened sinner's heart.' Ah, yes! dear fellow-sinner, *something can*. If God speaks to you, *then* you will feel, and your heart will begin to break, and your eyes begin to weep. Oh! that God would speak home to your conscience. If any of you feel that he is doing so, harden not your hearts.

Again, *Sinning against light* hardens the heart. Persisting in any course of sin, or in any habits of sin, and yielding to temptation when conscience and the Word of God clearly and distinctly point out to you that what you are doing is wrong, opposed to the will of God, and in direct disobedience to his law. Nothing hardens the heart more than sin, felt to be sin, and yet persisted and delighted in.

Further, *The rejection of Christ* hardens the heart. Indeed, nothing is so hardening as the rejection of Immanuel. True, it does not make *his* heart the less full of love to you, or the less willing to receive you. Ah, no! for though you have kept him waiting long, he is waiting still. But every fresh call to come to Christ, every new offer of mercy that you reject, just adds another link to the chain with which Satan binds you, and makes it the less probable that you will ever be taken from his grasp.

Have I received Christ, or am I rejecting him? Answer this to yourselves. You say, 'Of course I am a Christian; I

acknowledge Christ as my Saviour; I have always done it.'
Friend! you deceive yourself. A faith *of course*, is no faith
at all. Have you received Christ, or are you rejecting him?
Perhaps you do not know what the term means. Were you
offered Christ on one hand, and everything else on the
other, would you take Christ before all, or part with him
and take the world? Do you love Christ or your earthly
possessions, your lands, your houses, the best? Which
would you part with? Would you part with your dearest
companion on earth sooner than give up Christ? Would
you part with father, mother, sister, brother, lands,
all, rather than part with HIM? If you would, then you
have taken Christ for your portion; you are not rejecting
him.

And are you trusting to Christ alone, or to duties half,
and half to Christ? If the latter, you are rejecting Christ.
Would you like, as I know some would, to have Christ for
your Priest, to satisfy divine justice, without having him
for your Prophet and King? If you would, you are rejecting Christ.

But what is it to receive Christ? To be willing to take
his righteousness for your whole salvation, to take him as
your Priest to plead for you, your Prophet to instruct and
guide you in the path of his commandments, and your
King to govern you by setting his throne in your heart—
that is to receive Christ. Are you doing this? Have you
ever done it? Are you willing to do it now? Ah! how little
value does the poor blind world set on Christ! Is there not
something marvellous in the little value sinners have for a
Saviour?

If you were told to-night that all the lands that surround your dwelling were your own, would not your
heart leap for joy? And yet there is a greater treasure

offered you to-night, full and free, not only for the asking, but for the mere will to receive it. Ah, yes! Christ, in whom are hid all the treasures of wisdom and knowledge, is offered to you. He knocks to-night, he asks you to open the door, and says, 'If any man hear my voice.' See the distinction again made here. *If any man hear* MY *voice.* Every one in this house hears the preacher's voice declaring in his ear the word of Jesus; but are any hearing his voice in their hearts? Is Jesus speaking to you, beloved friends? If he be, harden not your hearts; for he says, 'If any man hear MY voice, *and open the door*, I will come in to him and sup with him, and he with me.' Who is yielding to Immanuel's still small voice of love? Which of you is saying, 'Come, Lord Jesus, come quickly?' Your heart is ever open to words of kindness, open to the voice of parent and friend, open to the love of a wife, a husband, a child, a brother, a sister; but, oh! it is closed against Immanuel. Why is it so? For what is so natural as that the heart of the creature should be open to the Creator, the heart of the sinner to the Saviour? Are we not to get one soul for Christ from your lovely glen? We would fain get one from these mountains. The scenes you dwell among are lovely scenes. The mountains and the valleys, the rocks that surround you, are beautiful indeed; but there is a sight that is lovelier still. No sight in the universe is half so lovely as the sight of a soul fleeing to Christ, coming with its whole burden of sin, casting it on him, and taking refuge, and finding safety in the everlasting arms. Open up to him these sealed hearts; let them go out towards him, and take him for your portion now and for ever. If you reject him now, the consequence *may* be, that the Spirit will no longer strive with you; or if, in infinite mercy, the offer be made to you a few times more, and you reject him still, the consequence *must* be, that you, through unbelief, shall not enter into his rest.

Before parting, we shall repeat in your hearing some of the words of God. Listen for once to God's own voice. There are souls present who, to this night have never once known what it is to listen with solemn awe to Jehovah, to that word which is law throughout the universe, law to angel and archangel, to winds, and waves, and storms, aye, and to the very devils in hell.

Believers! will you now begin to pray for the outpouring of the Spirit, that before we part it may be granted, and that many souls may yet tonight be given to Christ.

The first word of God which we shall repeat, is this— '*Ye must be born again.*' What think ye of this? Man, woman, child, are you born again? The words, 'ye must be born again,' *mean something*. What *do* they mean? They are either to be rejected as foolish, vain words, without any meaning whatsoever, or they have a meaning that some of you wish they had not, an awful meaning; for they say that you are lost. What language could Jehovah use to convince you of that truth, stronger than the language he has used— ye *must* be born again. *You must*, old hardened sinner; *you* must, young beginner in sin; *you* must, that are rich; you that are poor; one and all, unless already regenerated. You *must* be born again. Now, what do you say to this? There are hundreds now before me that know nothing of the new birth but the name; many who rejoice that the people in this neighbourhood have too much common sense to join the weak, woman-hearted men, who in other places are

49

weeping for their sins, and joining themselves to their Saviour; many who laugh at conversion, and call it all vain talk, and hate the very name of saint.

But there is another class to which we would speak, those who expect to be saved because, say they, 'We know we are Christians, and what more would you have?' They are good neighbours, kind to those poorer than themselves; they do their duty, and think it the height of uncharitableness in any one to hint at their not being Christians. My dear friends, have you ever known a thorough change of heart? No! and yet you are quite at ease. Then yours is truly an awful case. In danger of hell every moment, and yet you are deceived. We know not what to say to you, to convince you that you are unsaved sinners. Christians! *you* have much to answer for, in the way you help to deceive these poor perishing souls. Ah, yes! in that day, many a one will be crying out to those Christians who have lived near them, and been much with them, without ever warning them of their danger; many a poor lost soul, believer, will be crying out to you, 'Why did you not warn me? *You* knew what my end was to be, and I didn't know it, and yet you never told me. Why did you let me rest before you had persuaded me, or driven me to flee to Christ for shelter from this storm of wrath?' We cannot bear to think of the multitudes who are daily settling down, at peace and sure of heaven, without a single warning word from Christians. Believe me, friends, there is nothing so fatal to a poor soul as, while unregenerate, *to be set down as a Christian*; above all, to be acknowledged as such *by* Christians.

Let no man's opinion be your warrant for heaven. Let your only warrant be a warrant taken from the clear declarations of the Word of God. One of the plainest of these is, *ye* must be born again. How little man will be satisfied with in a fellow-creature! A man happens to be stamped a Christian at some period of life; he at least believes that he is one; he goes on measuring and measuring his practice, his conduct, his words, with the short crooked line of a fellow-creature's corrupt example, or the low deficient standard set up by fallen man. He never thinks of trying himself by the measuring line of the sanctuary. You think, perhaps, that ministers are all Christians; and that none require to live so much to Christ as ministers do. Leave that to Rome and the apostasy—leave *her* to speak of priest and of pope, but give ye glory to the Lamb, who hath made you all kings and priests to God. There is not a poor saint among you, that may not join with the Redeemer in ascribing eternal praise that *he* or *she* is made a priest to the living God, to offer to him sacrifice continually in the land where there is no temple. Ah! but every minister is not a priest to God. People seem to think that entering the church converts a man, that he is born again when he enters the sacred office. But it is not educating a man for the ministry, it is not sending a man to college, and putting a gown on his back, and putting him into a pulpit, that will make him a Christian. There is many a minister that is not a Christian; many a learned expositor of Jehovah's word, whom that word will never save; and many a one who says to you, '*If ye shall hear His voice,*' who never yet himself heard the voice of God.

Then, by man's way of estimating, there is much less religion needed in a rich man than in a poor man to make him a Christian. Very little, indeed, will do in a marquis, a duke, or earl; a very little *patronage to religion* from one such, sets him down to be a Christian. And how little will do in a landlord! If a landlord sometimes says a word to you about the fear of God, if he is known to read the Bible, and to go to church, he's a Christian, there's no doubt about it; indeed, to appear at a humble prayer-meeting, would be a thing too much to expect from him, even as a Christian.

This is the ruin of many in the higher ranks. If a young person, for instance, has been the subject of impressions, and sees it right to retire a little from the world, and thus comes under the notice of gay companions as one who is going to become a saint, he or she gets the name for a very small outward profession, and is at once marked as a Christian; and, having got the name, is received by Christians at once as such. And, though at first the individual may be very doubtful as to his or her *claim* to the reality of the name, a title to it becomes so easily confirmed by the opinions of other Christians, and especially that of Christian ministers, that the individual at length becomes quite at rest on the point of his being indeed a Christian; and when that point is once settled in a man's mind, and when the consistent discharge of outward duty appears as its fruit, I can tell you that it is not *man's word* that will convince such an one that he is still a child of wrath. Ah, no! you cannot conceive how a man's heart gets hedged in, and in, and in, and round, and round; while every year that is unstained by the commission of gross iniquity—nay, perhaps adorned by a series of actions that present a fair face to the eye of the community— sears his deceived heart till it becomes impervious to conviction, and, as it were, sets him beyond the mark of man's arrows. We can't get at you, consistent, sober, honest, amiable professor, hypocrite at ease in Zion! We can't say a word to you to which we shall not get a scriptural answer; everything we say falls on this side of you. 'We like that preaching,' you say, 'it's honest, it's plain; I hope my neighbour took that word to himself, it suited him; that sermon was well fitted to arouse the sleeping.' Oh! that we heard you saying, 'It suited *me*, it suited me.' Blessed be God, the most secure among you is not out of the reach of the arrows of the Mighty One. No, sinner, if the omnipotent Spirit of Jehovah shoots at you but one arrow, you will not escape; you will quail, you will fall, and cry for mercy and pardon—not for this man, or for that man, but to ME, a sinner.

Do not seek to cover up your sins with the varnish of hypocrisy, the fine gloss that pleases men. Men-pleasers! men-followers! the flames of judgment will melt the varnish on your fair faces, and make it run down, till the black hideous deformity be made visible to an astonished universe. Cast it all away now, and come as poor burdened ones to receive mercy.

Some of you scoff at the call to turn. All we can get from you is, 'Not yet, not yet.' The oldest among you says 'Not yet.' Young men say, 'Not yet, not yet; we are too young to be made saints of; life is short, we may surely take the good of our youth. You would not have us spend our bright, light-hearted days in weeping and mourning; you wouldn't put us yet into the strait-jacket of a Christian's scruples, or oppress us with the weight of the Christian's cross.' Dear young friends, there are many of your own age, who could tell you that when a soul has cast its own yoke on Christ, he makes it feel his yoke easy, his burden light. There are young men and young women in other places, who, at no distant period have taken up that cross, and found that Christ, as he laid it on them, at the same time, as it were, took off the weight of it, by bearing it along with them. And now they go rejoicing all the day in the God of their salvation.

You are not too young to be lost; not too young to fall into the galling, soul-and-body-binding, chains of Satan's prison-house; not too young to be shut up with devils in the pit. Just because life is short, I entreat you to join yourselves to Jesus. Stop and think! Stop and tremble!

Hear now another word of God, the last to which we shall direct your attention. 'Come now, and let us reason together, saith Jehovah: though your sins be as scarlet, they shall be as white as snow; though they be red like crimson, they shall be as wool.' Have you ever believed that? Heard it you have, times without number; but have you received it; have you set to your seal, that God is true when he speaks thus? And when the devil, or your own heart, has tempted you to disbelieve this, by saying that your sins are too many to be pardoned, thus giving God the lie, have you said, 'I will abide by this: let God be true, and every man—every opposer of his truth whether man, or devil, or my own heart—*a liar.*'

If you have thought, that in speaking to you this night, we have been wanting in tenderness, believe that it is, so to speak, against our will. All night we could speak on to you of the love of Christ, for it is boundless, fathomless, unsearchable, inexhaustible, an endless theme for saved sinners here, an endless theme for the glorified above; but however hard for us to speak or you to hear, we *must* tell you the whole truth, and *speak it out.* Let this word of the living God make up for all want of tenderness in man: 'Though your sins be as scarlet, they shall be white as snow.' Glorious words to be repeated in a poor sinner's ear! And we would say to you, who may have been led by the Spirit for the first time this night to hear the Word of God; who can no longer hold out against the truth of the former words of God, repeated in your hearing, but who are now convinced of sin; that you must no more harden your hearts at this declaration of love, than you must when, in the light of the Spirit, you bend to the truth that you must be born again, created anew in Christ Jesus.

No verse in this book seems more fitted to affect the heart of the sin-burdened soul, than this full, unconditional declaration of a free pardon. If terror will not move you, then cry out in wonder, 'Who is a God like unto thee that pardoneth?' Nor can you bring out one sin, dear fellow sinner, which may not be completely sunk out of remembrance in the ocean depths of love. You say your sins are many. Listen to Immanuel's voice—'Thy sins, which are many, are forgiven.' They are of crimson dye. That shews you are the very person Jehovah invites to 'Come and reason.' They rise in mountain height around you; the prospect is darkened; it is the night of death and despair! Then *you* are *the* sinner God invites. A crimson sinner, a scarlet sinner, a black sinner of the darkest shade! God knew that you would be made to feel that; he knew that no less than an invitation, a free welcome, a joyous reception, to a crimson sinner, would suffice to reassure your unbelieving, distrustful heart, and he tells you that your sins shall be made white as snow. In Christ there is merit to justify the most hell-deserving of our race.

If any among you are now so weighed down under a sense of sin, that you cannot look up, we praise God on your behalf. Happy, happy are you! Happy souls that are trying to convince God that your sins are too black to be washed out, that your load is too heavy to be removed! The God of love will convince you that he *can* justify you, and yet be just. Happy souls, that are lying at his footstool, and reasoning thus, 'Lord, I cannot ask for mercy. Oh, my sins, my sins!' The God of love will open your eyes, and shew you a fountain flowing on Calvary that can cleanse such as you, a robe of righteousness that can cover you, *so cover you*, that his own eye shall rest on you with delight, as it rests on the imputed righteousness that shines upon you. Ah, yes! when the Spirit shall have fully convinced you of sin, and fully shewn you the depravity of your own heart, he will convince you of righteousness, a righteousness that is divine. We leave with you, mourners, a passage in Isaiah 30. 18, 'And therefore will the Lord wait, that he may be gracious unto you; and therefore will he be exalted, that he may have mercy upon you: for the Lord is a God of judgment: blessed are all they that wait for him. For the people shall dwell in Zion at Jerusalem; thou shalt weep no more: he will be very gracious unto thee at the voice of thy cry; when he shall hear it, he will answer thee.'

4

I AM DEBTOR

[*Preached November 28th 1841, in Edinburgh, to the Congregation of the Rev. A. Moody Stuart, then absent in Madeira, whose place Burns supplied.*]

'I AM DEBTOR BOTH TO THE GREEKS, AND TO THE BARBARIANS; BOTH TO THE WISE, AND TO THE UNWISE.'—*Romans 1. 14.*

Paul had a strong desire, as it appears from the context of these words, to convince the Church of Rome of two things: first, of his own commission to preach the gospel; and second, that he had a very warm heart towards themselves—not only that he had a call to preach to them, but a very fervent desire to do this work. 'Often-times I purposed to come unto you, (but was let hitherto), that I might have some fruit among you also, even as among other Gentiles.' One reason he had already given; he longed to impart to the believers there some spiritual gift, to the end they might be established. But although he expresses this desire, and although the work of establishing believers in the faith is one of the chief obligations laid on every minister of Christ, yet there was no man less willing than Paul to build on another man's foundation; and, therefore, he greatly desired to have some fruit among the Romans as well as among the other Gentiles. He had got many a bright gem among the heathen, but he earnestly desired some jewels for his crown of glory from among this people. This desire was very natural to one who had such a warm heart towards the cause and kingdom of the Lord Jesus as had the Apostle: his heart had learned to stretch itself forth to embrace, in the bowels of Jesus Christ, the whole lost world.

We behold in Paul, a notable example of zeal for the Master's cause, a very different thing from the zeal of corrupt nature. There *is* such a thing as zeal in the natural heart, and it can sometimes exist in a human cause for a long life, without apparent abatement or declension; but true zeal is quite different from this, and is only to be found in a child of God. It cannot stand, or breathe, or act, or move, far less *endure*, except in so far as Christ himself breathes, and acts, and moves in the soul. To believers now, it is indeed a wonderful sight to look back to the grace that Paul got in this respect, and to see how zealous, active, and persevering he was in the Lord's service.

Yet, while looking back to Paul, let us be careful to remember that it is not in ministers alone that this zeal should be found. It is just as much the part and the character of *private* Christians to be very jealous for the honour of the Lord of hosts. There is much zeal in the world, and there is nothing so easy or so pleasing to the natural man as to be zealous in a cause, the glory of which is to revert to himself; so much so, that Christ tells us of the Pharisees, that they would compass sea and land to make one proselyte, who, when gained over, they made twofold more the child of hell than themselves. We have had many a proof of this, in the exertions made since the days of the Pharisees, by men who have had the Pharisees' spirit. How much will they do, how much will they give, how much sea and land will they compass to make a few proselytes! Even to the Jews, Paul bore witness that they had a zeal of God, though not according to knowledge. Therefore, my dear friends, you must search out your hearts well, and bring your motives to the light; for we know that zeal for the spread of any merely human opinion, or even for the spread of any spiritual truth, which is not of a primary kind, is no evidence that we are of the number of God's people. A zeal to gain over men to argue on doctrines, so dark and incomprehensible, perhaps, that God has seemed to place them on a secondary scale, and to the belief of which he has evidently not called all men; a great and mistaken zeal for the spread of particular doctrines or tenets, or of peculiar views, or of sects—does exist, without having grace for the spring of it. But there can be no true zeal, having the glory of God and the salvation of sinners for its only aim, without the grace of God in the soul. Oh! how much would be done for God, if his true servants had as much zeal in his holy cause, as professors often have in the propagation of some peculiar opinion.

We come now to the *mainspring* and reason of all Paul's zeal for the Romans and all other Gentiles. 'I am debtor both to the Greeks and to Barbarians; both to the wise and to the unwise. So, as much as in me is, I am ready to preach the gospel to you that are at Rome also.' I AM DEBTOR. What is his meaning here? Does Paul mean by this, that the Gentiles had done anything for him? some services that merited return? No; for though he might have laid claim to much as the due reward of his services, he determined to be chargeable to no man; and he says, 'Though I be free from all men, yet have I made myself servant unto all, that I might gain the more.' How was he, then, their debtor? He was so on two grounds. The first of these was, *the state in which the Gentiles were*. The second, *Christ's dealings with himself*. He was debtor to the Gentiles, because he saw the whole Gentile world lying in sin, condemned, depraved, enslaved, carried away captive by the devil at his will, disobedient, and so under the curse of God. This was one thing that brought Paul under a debt, a vast debt of obligation to them, so that he could say, 'I am debtor both to the Greeks and to the Barbarians.' How so? Because he was not like Cain, saying, 'Am I my brother's keeper?' The gospel taught him, on the contrary, to love his neighbour as himself. He deeply realised that since the Lord had freely saved *him*, he was bound to be as tender and compassionate for others as of his own soul. How strongly he felt it towards the Jews, these wonderful words bear witness, 'Brethren, my heart's desire and prayer to God for Israel is, that they might be saved.' 'I say the truth in Christ, I lie not, my conscience also bearing me witness in the Holy Ghost, that I have great heaviness and continual sorrow in my heart. For I could wish that myself were accursed from Christ for my brethren, my kinsmen according to the flesh.'

We learn from this, that all Christians are debtors to those who are without Christ; that they should be moved by compassion for a perishing world, to go forward with this as their prevailing motive, that through grace they have become debtors to *all men*. And if this be binding on every follower of Christ, how much more on ministers of the everlasting gospel? Oh! that they felt it more. If we had but more of the grace of God, we should. When ministers have little grace, they cannot feel this, just because they do not see the danger of others. They see men more in the light of being inhabitants of the world, than as going on with speed to death, to judgment, and to hell.

But ah! where a true minister of Christ does get a view of the lost condition of mankind, he cannot get over it. A heavy weight lies on his bosom, which nothing can remove. He has great desires after the salvation of the soul, and cannot rest without pulling sinners out of the fire, while hating the garment spotted with the flesh. Thus he becomes debtor to the whole world.

But the thought of what Christ had done for him, as well as the peculiar way in which he had called him, made Paul feel this. Even at the time of his conversion, the Lord had told him that he was a chosen vessel for this end; making him to know that he was converted for the very purpose of bringing souls to Immanuel. He got his commission as an ambassador of Christ at the very time he received a pardon. His charge to declare the gospel of Jesus was written, as it were, on the same parchment with his own pardon—written on the very charter of his salvation. Every way he was bound and obliged to preach the gospel. Not as a condition of his pardon. God forbid! Ah, no, it was all from love, love to God and man. He had nothing left to glory in, the utmost he could ever do, could not acquit the debt of love. It was laid on him as a solemn duty by the God of salvation, so that he was not only constrained to preach, but to say, 'Woe is me if I preach not the gospel.' This feeling of imperative obligation to declare the truth, did not belong to Paul alone; every man that has the grace of God within him feels it. There is no such thing as a monopoly of grace; her language and her charge to all is, 'Freely ye have received, freely give.' 'And the Spirit and the bride say, Come, And let *him that heareth* say, Come. And let him that is athirst come. And whosoever will, let him take the water of life freely.' Like the woman of Samaria, who left her waterpot and returned into the city, and told them that were in it to come and see a man who had told her all that ever she did; so we see that when one hears of Christ, he tells another, and brings another, too. A man is bound to do it—he cannot help it—he cannot contain it within him; a necessity is laid on his spirit, and woe be to him if he preach not the gospel.

The apostle says something more than this—'I am debtor both to the Greeks, and to the Barbarians; both to the wise, and the unwise.' The meaning of this seems to be: if I were free to make a *choice*, I might choose the Barbarian or I might choose the Greek, I might choose the wise or the unwise; but Paul says, *I am debtor*, and a debtor has no such thing as a choice to make in regard to whom he will pay his debts. The debtor knows this, and the believer feels it just in the same way: 'Whatever my calculations may be, or whatever I might myself desire, the question is not, *what would I like*? but *what is my commission*? what are the objects of my embassy? It is not *my choice* that I have to do with, but *God's commission*; what instructions does it contain?'

We would fain impress this important, solemn truth upon God's children. Believer, do you feel this? Do you know what it is to feel yourself a debtor to a lost world? Have you ever thought of what object Christ had in view when he brought you to himself? what design he had in calling you? It was certainly, in the first instance, to save you from perdition, but that was not the only end. It is possible to think too much, or, at least, too exclusively, about your own case. In one sense you cannot do that; woe be to him who seeks to pull the mote out of a brother's eye,

when a beam is in his own. But yet a believer must remember that he is called to know Christ, not only to be
safe himself, but also that he may be a witness for Christ in
the world. Ah! think of this; don't be selfish in the matter
of salvation, and remember above all, that this is not a
thing which you may or may not do, just as you like. Some
people do much in this way, just because they have a liking
to it, and because the employment suits their taste; and it
is a happy thing to feel that; but there is a far more unchangeable foundation for a believer's labour in the Lord's
vineyard than that. The man is no longer free to like, or
not to like; he is a debtor now—a debtor to do it fully, and
constantly, and unceasingly, and devotedly, whether he
likes it or not. Think of it in this light, and then you will be
going and hasting to tell your friends, and all whom you
know, of these precious things of God. Oh, if this were
fully felt, and felt universally, how many would be preaching whose mouths are dumb through sloth and idleness!
There would be fewer preaching as a trade, and more
preaching as debtors, for every believer would then have a
voice with which to sound the praises of the most high
God.

There is often a very great mistake made in this way
among believers when speaking of one another. They say,
How much such and such a one does for God and for
souls! seeming to think that it is a great grace in that man;
whereas the truth is, that when once a man becomes a
Christian, his ceasing to declare Christ is a very fearful
shortcoming in simple duty. The command is to preach
the gospel, and to cease from it is disobedience. The
obligation is to preach the gospel, and how dare he be
silent? A minister is just as guilty if he cease from this, as if

he left an earthly debt unpaid. For instance, such an obligation is laid on me as one of Christ's ministers. Now, it is not in the least left to my choice whether or not I am to preach continually the gospel of Christ. The world can claim it, believers can claim it, woe, woe is me if I preach not the gospel! As to my liking it, that is another thing; if my heart is with the work, then I shall have my reward. See the fulfilment of this when God gives the commandment for it—

> *The Lord himself did give the word,*
> *The word abroad did spread;*
> *Great was the company of them,*
> *The same who published.*

If we are to be useful in God's vineyard, we must not take it into our own hands to direct how or where we are to do his work. We must not go upon our own conjectures, but walk by God's rule. O that we all felt that we had no liberty in this matter! When once a man has given himself to God, he has given away all right to this. It *is* left to a man's own choice whether he will give his heart to Christ or not; but when he has given his heart to Christ, it is *not* left to his own choice whether he will shine as a light in the world or not.

If the believer be a debtor, he is bound continually to seek opportunity to speak to those around him, that he may win them to the Lord. We are very apt to make a choice in this, but, ah! guard against it, if you would get the blessing. Did you never feel, in giving away a tract, or in speaking to any one, as if you had a choice in the matter? You felt as if in one case you were likely to succeed, and not in the other. This is a great error, and may keep you from doing much good. If such be the duty of all Christians, how careful should elders and teachers be to be instant in the work committed to them.

Believer, have *you* no ungodly companion, whom you might try to bring to the knowledge of God? Remember, you are a debtor, and bound to do it. How many there are who, even if they instruct their children, yet neglect their servants. In how many houses, where godliness is professed have the servants never had a question directly put to their consciences, that might awaken them!

There is fearful guilt lying on the heads of many in this matter; and why is there so great an unwillingness to anything of the kind? Just because if masters were to do this, it would have two effects. They would themselves require to live very consistently, to watch their own actions, and guard their own words and looks in the presence of their servants; and a second effect would be, that there would be many more of the inmates of such households brought to Christ, attracted by holy conversation, and their likeness to Christ. Ah! if parents lived thus holily before their children, there would be another effect; it would be this, that they would not so often go down to the grave leaving unconverted children behind them in the world; or, what is as bad, if they do live, seeing the ruin of sons and daughters given over to vanity and folly. If parents took this more to heart, it would save them many a pang, and many a dark hour.

And neighbours have also a duty belonging to them, too often, alas, forgotten. How few think it necessary to speak a word to an unconverted neighbour, although they know they are guilty in being silent. What excuse do they give? 'Oh, that it would be meddling, and interfering with other people's matters.' And so it would be meddling, unless you did it from love to Christ. But, my dear friends, if you were to do it, and to do it in a kind, humble, and gentle way, your neighbours, however bad they might be, would thank you for taking a kind interest in them. Oh, be jealous of your motives for silence, for there seems to be about some Christians so much restraint and coldness, that if a neighbour or acquaintance were willing to receive instruction from them, he could hardly get it.

Were you never ashamed, in some companies, to recognise Christ as your Master? You love to wear the white robe in private, or even, perhaps, in the family; but ah! it is far too white to walk with in the world: it would give you too much singularity of appearance there. Sad it is, when a believer is ashamed, in any point, of the gospel of Christ. Were you never tempted, when giving tracts away, to distribute them among the poor; yet to be disinclined to give them to the rich, thinking them less likely to get good; and did you never, when you had overcome the false shame, find that the unlikely person was the only one who got good? Did you never feel as if the devil were tempting you back from those very acts which God has been afterwards pleased most graciously to bless? We speak from self-experience; for often have we been left, especially in the preaching of the gospel, to regret having chosen for ourselves. The place to which we may have gone with the greatest repugnance, thinking that, from some circumstance, the probabilities of success were small, has been the very one where God has helped us. It may not be gratifying to our fallen nature to believe it, but what we have to learn is, to do the work of servants, and not, as we might choose, the work of masters. Let every Christian remember, in conclusion, that he is a debtor; a debtor to the Lord Jesus Christ; a debtor to a fallen world.

And now, unconverted fellow-sinners, do not these

considerations, which we have sought to impress on the minds and bind on the consciences of believers, apply very forcibly, if indirectly, to you? Is it no proof of the love of God towards you, that he has made all his true people feel that they are debtors to you, that they may bring you to the knowledge of Christ Jesus? Many a debt you owe to God, though you never dreamed of trying to pay one of them. And yet he has not only counselled, and besought, and commanded his quickened people to take every means in their power to turn you; but he has laid on them a woe, if each one of them do not, in his different sphere and way, preach the gospel to you. Is it not wonderful that, as soon as they believe the gospel themselves, they cry out under the weight of a fearful responsibility lying on their souls, 'I am debtor both to the Greeks and to the Barbarians; both to the wise and to the unwise'?

Every converted soul, from the hour of its conversion, is commissioned to seek and to save that which was lost. Try, then, to praise the Lord for this. Try to wonder at his goodness, that, instead of taking his dear children home, when first they come to him, he leaves them in a world of enemies, that they may seek for you. He might transplant them at once to their eternal, blessed home with himself in glory, as soon as they had tasted of his love; but he leaves them amid sorrow and trial, in a vale of tears, that they may be ensamples to you, as Christ is to them; nay, more, he lays woe upon them if they preach not the gospel. Ah! how much easier for them if, as soon as they could call him FATHER, they were to reach their Father's house, and get the smile of his reconciled countenance—if, as soon as their souls were lighted at the Spirit's fire, they were allowed to burst forth into the flame of glory, with which redeemed souls shine in the kingdom above, instead of having to shine so dimly, as at best they do, while only lights in a world that knows them not? Yes, but *what would the world be without them?*

5

THE SECRET PLACE

[Preached in St Leonard's Church, Perth, February 8, 1842. The visits which Burns paid to Perth, from time to time, were eagerly looked forward to by the converts there and in the neighbourhood. On each of these occasions, the church was crowded long before the time; careless relatives and acquaintances were led by believers to listen to the voice which had been the means of calling themselves to the feet of Jesus. Such was the affection entertained for Burns by the many young men of Perth who had been thus blessed, that, on the night preceding his appearance before the Presbytery of Aberdeen— the hostile party of which sought to deprive him of licence—they spent the night in prayer, that God would overrule all for his glory, and uphold his young servant.]

'COME, MY PEOPLE, ENTER THOU INTO THY CHAMBERS, AND SHUT THY DOORS ABOUT THEE: HIDE THYSELF, AS IT WERE, FOR A LITTLE MOMENT, UNTIL THE INDIGNATION BE OVERPAST. FOR BEHOLD, THE LORD COMETH OUT OF HIS PLACE TO PUNISH THE INHABITANTS OF THE EARTH FOR THEIR INIQUITY: THE EARTH ALSO SHALL DISCLOSE HER BLOOD, AND SHALL NO MORE COVER HER SLAIN.'—*Isaiah 26. 20, 21.*

Read in connection, Exodus 12. 22, 23. Notice here, first, A duty enjoined, and also a particular occasion for this duty, arising from that which God is about to do. Such an exhortation is always suitable; but it is specially so at those times when appearances arise of God's displeasure being poured out against a people and against a kingdom; and when a nation's cup of guilt is so filled up to the brim as to be ready to run over.

'Come, my people, enter into thy chambers.' Three views may be taken of this word, one agreeing with that text in Matthew: 'And thou, when thou prayest, enter into thy closet,' etc. And, again, it may be understood in the sense of the passage read from Exodus, which tells of the blood being sprinkled on the posts and the lintels of the doors; and also in the light of those passages which speak of God as a hiding-place: 'He shall hide them in the secret of his presence;' etc. These views, however, express the same thing. Entering into the 'secret place' is only useful in so far as we enter thereby into the secret of God's pavilion; and it is only by entering into the secret of God's pavilion that his people can ever be safe from their enemies.

Now when do we enter into the secret of God's pavilion? How do we enter there? We come to the Holy God, as to one who is a Spirit, possessed of infinite perfections, the just, true, and gracious God. His presence is called *the Holiest of all*. This expression denotes, perhaps, the nearest possible approach to God.

How do we come to him? By the blood of the covenant; and with all boldness.

Now I fear we often think that we can come without this blood; or rather without any deep sense of our need of it. But what is the reason of that? Simply that some of us do not know God at all; and that we never yet have discovered either our enmity to God, or God's contrariety to us.

Now, beloved friends, the very first effect which the knowledge of God has upon a man, is to make him feel that he is full of enmity to God, and that therefore he cannot and dare not come to God. He trembles at the very mention of his name: he never can hear it with joy until he has been sprinkled by the blood. This approach by Christ's blood is clearly shewn forth in the passover. The blood on the lintel kept the destroying angel out. This is just a picture of the covenant of grace. Sprinkled with this blood, we can draw near to God. It is not natural to fallen man to come near in this way, and it is only when sin is weakened within us, that we can do so. But when God by his Spirit draws us, then we come by his way, and have boldness to enter into the Holiest of all.

But then, remember, that makes us humble. No soul that ever entered there remained proud, either toward God or man: and this just belies the approaches to God that some people say they make. If they find it a natural and easy thing to come into the secret of his presence; if they find that their nature goes quite along with it, and they can enter there at all times, without difficulty; this proves nothing but their ignorance of God.

The effect of the least knowledge of God's blessed perfections, is to drive a man to the blood of Christ, and to make him set a high value on that precious blood. *Now* it is that, this blood having been applied afresh to the conscience, he comes a poor, rebellious, God-dishonouring sinner, to present on the altar his body and soul a living sacrifice.

Again, when a believer goes into his secret place, he requires to have this blood of sprinkling applied to his conscience, and that blood he presents to God. But before he can do this, the enmity must be slain by the power of God's Spirit: and this is one of the tokens of God's eternal covenant with his Son having been ratified, that the believer feels this within him, as one of its glorious fruits.

True, the enmity is only so far slain; it is not yet extinct. Believers know this: and when we come into our secret place, do we not often bring with us that awful distance of heart, which dwells even in God's own people? It can never be destroyed while sin remains in them, and it can only be subdued by the sprinkling of the blood of the Lamb.

Now, if there are any present who never have known what enmity is; and who find it quite an easy matter to come before him in prayer at all times, what does this prove? That they are living near to God? It just proves this, that such people know nothing of God.

It is when a man meets for the first time with God as a righteous God in Christ, and when God at the same time meets with the sinner as a returning and believing child, saying, Abba Father, that the sinner is reconciled to God, and united to the Saviour.

And what follows? Only the same thing again and again till his dying day. The duty of Christ's religion is in fact just this, that the believing sinner cannot help coming from day to day, and coming always newly, and yet always in the same way, to his reconciled God and Father in Christ Jesus.

We have dwelt on this, because it is ever to this same daily duty of coming to himself in Christ, that God directs men, when he is about to call them to trial and suffering, and would prepare them to endure such.

This is the only preparation that a believer needs when days of persecution are at hand, or when they actually arrive. It is not some new, unheard of thing that they need, some new duty they are called to. Ah, no! blessed be God. Or if you call it new, it is only in this sense, that it is to be performed with new zeal, with new strength, with new desires of attaining to the enjoyments of God. So that when he says to his people, 'Come, my people, enter into thy chambers,' he is just calling them to closer communion with himself; to more frequent coming to the blood of Christ than before, that they may become more lively members of a living Head.

If we do not make this blessed use of communion with God; if we do not use God's perfections as a refuge and a hiding-place, then prayer is useless to us; it must be a first step to the secret of God's presence. This has been the refuge of God's people in every age.

We entreat you to cultivate secret prayer. Oh! seek never to enter the secret place without going into the presence of the Holy One, to have dealings with the Lord God. Taste the sweetness of casting yourself by faith upon the perfections of God as reconciled in the cross, for your only refuge, with Christ's sinless obedience as your covering in his sight.

And it is just by obedience to this very command that every justified sinner is sanctified and prepared for a state of glory, and perfected by degrees into complete conformity to the image of Immanuel.

Ah, yes! beloved, and it is by this very process, humbling as it is, that *you*, believer, are to be strengthened and emboldened, and prepared for times of trial, of suffering, and of death.

And in the day which is coming, a day of wrath, a day of trouble and distress, 'a day of darkness and of gloominess, a day of clouds and of thick darkness;' what will you need then? When the cup of a nation's sin is filled up, and when 'the Lord cometh out of his place to punish the inhabitants of the earth for their iniquity,' what will you need? Just what you have been needing all the while: to be hidden in the secret place of the Most High God!

If you wish in that day to be secure, under the covert of your holy, holy, holy God, from the storm of the Lord's anger, then you must be much in the Lord's presence. This must become more precious to you than it is, and then you will better understand the duty, as well as the privilege, of entering into your chamber and shutting to the door, until his indignation be overpast. Alas! when times of trial come, many die away, and fall back, and are burned by the scorching rays of persecution, just because they never got power to come to God, and take refuge in him from all danger.

But let us not forget to say, that many who do come into the secret place, and who are God's children, enter it and leave it just as they entered, without ever so much as realising the presence of God.

And there are some believers who, even when they do obtain a blessing, and get a little quickening of soul, leave the secret place without seeking more. They go to their chamber, and there get into the secret place, but then, as soon as they have got near to him, they think they have been peculiarly blessed, and leave their chamber, and go back into the world.

Now this is calculated to draw us back again into sin: at least, by this we may lose many glorious advantages that we might otherwise gain over it. It is just by perseverance in prayer that we get the shelter we need.

Fix your minds upon this, that in the coming Day what will constitute safety will not be the profession of godliness, though that be good in itself; not zeal for Christ's cause, not *anything* but the being hid in the secret of God, and a more solemn, secret, personal, sensible union, or rather confirming of the union between the believer and Christ.

We know that in such times many shall be blown away as the chaff, who were not so esteemed before: and the reason will be, that they were not acquainted with the Holy God with whom they have to do. Beware, believers, of this; try yourselves by this balance of the sanctuary, that you be not judged of the Lord.

Oh! how is it that the Lord's own people have so little perseverance? How is it that when they do enter into their place of prayer to be alone, they are so easily persuaded to turn empty away; instead of wrestling with God to pour out his Spirit, they retire from the secret place without the answer, and submit to it *as being God's will*.

We must not let the evil deepen, until we sink into a state of backsliding; or make up our minds to bear it, or withdraw to some believer and talk about it, and then rest in a hope that we are living, just because we seem to feel that we are dead. This is a melancholy view of the case; and yet, believer, can you not bear witness to its truth in your inmost conscience, that there have been times when your complaining to others of deadness was a real comfort to yourself, and a sort of satisfactory proof to you that you were really alive unto God?

That is a husky, shallow religion, which leads you to be always going to ministers to complain of your deadness, instead of taking it to God, and lying with it all about you before the mercy-seat; casting your dead soul before him, doing violence to your sloth, and wrestling humbly, but earnestly, till you find an entrance into his holy presence.

Many are active enough in labour, and try to *do* much for God, as they think, but as to their prayers, where are they? Few indeed, and often dead enough! You go through them as a necessity, but they are soon over. But what does

God say? 'This is the will of God, even your sanctification.'

That blessed work would advance more rapidly, if, instead of laying the case before a friend or minister, you were rather keeping it to yourselves, and lying at God's feet till you conquer in his strength, and then contending with the pride which is growing out of the victory.

I read lately, in the life of an eminent servant of God, an incident illustrative of this. He was in the ministry, and one day two of his brethren came from a long distance to see him. To their surprise, he received them coldly, and would scarcely speak to them. When they saw this, they took leave, and as they were going, instead of asking them to remain, he bade them farewell, saying, 'You will wonder at the reception you have met with to-day; but I have been two hours this morning seeking access to God, and have not obtained it, and I have much need to be alone.'

This was one of the mighty wrestlers of the last century, who stirred up themselves to lay hold on Jehovah's strength; like the widow before the unjust judge, taking no denial, but, by their continual importunity, getting power with God, and prevailing.

If you dwelt in his presence you would be pressing forward to gaze on his holy perfections as so many chambers of safety for your souls. You would look on his power as your defence against the enemy. You would hide in his omnipotence, you would repose in his faithfulness, you would live upon his love, and take refuge in his very holiness, made yours in Christ Jesus. Strange refuge this for a guilty sinner! You would not be content with a mere knowledge *about* God. You would know Him as I AM THAT I AM. You would hear a voice say, 'Come, my people, come and make my perfections your refuge, and my presence your dwelling-place: make me your fortress, your buckler, your high tower.' You would be found studying his character as revealed in his Son; getting fresh discoveries of the glory of Christ, learning the worth of the atoning blood, and the depths of his unchanging love; daily crying out with him of old, 'Wash thou me.' And you would be daily going more out of self and into Immanuel, 'in whom we have redemption through his blood, the forgiveness of sins according to the riches of his grace.'

No man, who is a stranger to the fountain opened for sin, can be a Christian. No one who is a stranger to religion in secret can be a Christian. No one who is without communion with the living God can be a Christian. No man who is not forsaking every known sin can be a Christian. No man who refuses to discover to be sin, that which God's Spirit in his word has discovered to be Christ-dishonouring, can be a Christian. No! sin cannot live in the chambers of God's people, it cannot be carried into the secret of his presence, it cannot be indulged in the Holiest of all. Those who are holding their idols to their hearts, and setting up their sins as stumblingblocks before their eyes, are not Christians, but hollow professors and self-deceivers. Where will they be in a day of trial, when false refuges are wholly swept away, when all that is not hid in the secret of his pavilion shall be devoured by the overflowing scourge? Friends, when God's wrath shall sweep over every place but one, and *that* the secret of His own pavilion, what will you do then, if you are not there, if you have not obeyed this invitation, 'Come, my people, enter into thy chambers, and shut thy doors about thee; hide thyself, as it were, for a little moment, until the indignation be overpast?'

In application of this subject, we call upon all of you who

are still strangers to God, to believe that his scourge will soon sweep over this earth. Some of you think you can be safe at a distance, without delight in him, or communion with him. Fellow-sinners, what will you feel at the day of judgment, when you find yourself so far from God that when you call he will not answer. Because, when he called you, you would not hear, but tried to hide in the darkness of your own mind, in the darkness of a dead world, and a deceitful devil, and so remained a stranger to his love.

Poor formalist! whither will you flee when you see him face to face? And you who are regarding iniquity in your heart, where will *you* turn to? Forms and ceremonies won't screen you from that tempest. They will not make a break-water to the billows of his wrath. Even the most scriptural and sound belief will be worthless to you, if you have not made it your own. What would a mere good creed be at the day of judgment? The visible church will be no covert then. What avails the union of a dead member to a living body, if it never was connected with the life-giving head? A profession will not shelter you from the glance of the eye of fire. You may profess Christ till death, as many have done before you, and never know his gospel as the power of God. You may rank among God's people, you may appear to belong to the sheep, even till the day when the sheep shall be separated from the goats, but no longer; you will be on the left hand then. You may pass for Christians among Christians, among men, and under the eye of ministers. You may pass for such before the session; the elders may add your name to the communion roll. Yes; sad though this may seem, it is too often the case, that men's hypocrisy eludes the eye of ministers, of elders, and of God's own people; and yet they are hypocrites still. Have you met with God who is light, and in whom is no darkness at all? Have you met with God through the sprinkling of the blood? Is his Holy Spirit within you, getting the mastery over sin, and the victory over temptation? Or are you cleaving to that which he is urging you, or once urged you, to cast away, even after you had promised, as in the sight of God, to forsake it?

Yes, you shun the light lest your deeds be made manifest, while you make a fair show before men, cleaving to sin in your heart, and yet coming to the people of God, and to the ministers of God, and asking concerning him. Truly you will have a fearful end: for God says of such, that 'every one which separateth himself from me, and setteth up his idols in his heart, and putteth the stumbling-block of his iniquity before his face, and cometh to a prophet to inquire of him concerning me; I the LORD will answer him by myself; and I will set my face against that man, and will make him a sign and a proverb, and I will cut him off from the midst of my people, and ye shall know that I am the Lord.'

Not union with the visible church, not a profession of godliness, not a form of religion, not prayers and fastings, not good works, not tears and repentance, will save the soul in the day when earth shall disclose her dead, and shall no more cover her slain. Nothing less than the shelter of Christ's blood, in the secret place of Jehovah, the pavilion of him who is Almighty, will cover the sinner then. But blessed be God, though judgment may overtake us in a false security, and surprise us in an imagined faith, with a hypocrite's hope, it cannot follow us to, or overtake us in, the secret of God's pavilion. Ah! the roaring lion cannot come under that shade; he cannot find you there, feeble believer! Death and hell cannot shoot their arrows within the veil. The law cannot bring its summons into the

Holiest of all, nor the avenger of blood pursue. And why? Because it is sprinkled with the blood of Jesus.

Death will soon be here. Since last we met, many, many have been summoned to the bar of judgment, and have got their sentence sealed; and we wait to hear the voice that is to call us to himself. Not knowing when we may again be permitted to entreat you to return to God, we would the more urgently plead with you to be reconciled to him now by his Son. Are you dealing with the blood of Christ? Do you only make use of it to keep you at a distance from God? or, as some do, to despise God and his law altogether? If so, you have never had it applied to you at all—never! Christ's blood avails nothing except in so far as it brings you near to the Father of your spirits. Christ's blood is just a holy path to a holy nature.

We would address a word of caution to God's people, and it is this. Always seek in religion to feel and realise more than you express to others. Do not dwell on past experiences, as it were to comfort yourselves under the want of present grace; or speak of the experience to others, when the grace is almost gone. Ah, beloved! if this be a snare to any of you, you have need to learn to say with Paul, 'This one thing I do; forgetting those things which are behind,' etc. Press toward the mark, not your mark, or any man's mark, but God's mark. And what is God's mark? Perfection: 'Be ye also perfect, even as your Father in heaven is perfect.' Have your eye fixed *there*. Some never look so high as God's mark.

Your faith has many a victory to gain. Faith is a battle, a mighty warfare. It is a fight against all that is natural to you, against everything around you—that you may live on Christ alone. Faith is a trampling upon all, a despising and hating of all that comes between you and a fully revealed

Christ, a suffering the loss of all things to win Christ, and be found in him.

Be not surprised to find obstructions in the walk of faith. You will find them every hour. It is no slight grasp that must be taken of the kingdom of heaven in order to make a man safe amid the ruin and the wreck of a perishing world. Believe me, it is not with folded hands and drowsy consciences, and hearts full of the cares of this life, but denying ourselves, taking up the cross, bearing the reproach, and by following the Lamb whithersoever he goeth, that we shall enter the kingdom.

Young men! I see multitudes of you around me, and I rejoice at it. Ah, brother! will you not give your heart to Christ now? If you are troubled and kept back by the fear of man, we entreat you to remember for your encouragement, that *God* is known in Zion's palaces for *a* refuge. These are the words of the royal psalmist, who knew well what it was to need a refuge, and to find it in his God in many a trying hour. Our God cannot be truly known, without becoming a refuge. He is willing this hour to lead you the first step to the secret place of his own pavilion. There, every one of his perfections is pledged to protect you; and if so, what have you to fear? What power can you fear when hidden in Omnipotence? What wisdom or what device of the enemy, when Christ is made unto you wisdom, and sanctification, and complete redemption, when your Counsellor shall be the mighty God?

He that dwelleth in the secret place of the Most High shall abide under the shadow of the Almighty. Come under the covert of the Rock of Ages, get your soul sheltered here, and rejoice at once in the knowledge of this: that the guiltiest creature may dwell in the holiest place without any injury to the character of God. Our great High Priest entered into the Holiest of all, and he carried in with him his own blood as an eternal sacrifice for sin; and he hath, by one offering, perfected for ever them that are sanctified. It is high time to get the mark of the blood of the Son of God upon your foreheads.

This is no season to be drawing back, when we see men, in defiance of God's commands, about to lay their hands on our beloved Sabbaths. Ah! who can contemplate such a probability without trembling, who can see these bulwarks of religion shaken, who can look to the dismantling of these blessed fortresses, which are truly the strongholds of Scotchmen? Who can see the ungodly, for the gain of a little money, approaching to attack the citadel, and not tremble? or quietly listen to the iron wheels that in their speed are trampling down the Fourth Commandment? Soon your privileges may pass away. You may yet be under a dead, world-serving ministry, who will sell the truth of God for a pulpit and a place, and sing to you a syren song on the road to the pit. Is the Lord's work going on among you? Are the fishers of men getting fruit of their labour? or are their nets only made heavy by the stones or worthless fish that are drawn up? Plead with the Lord for Scotland. Ask that the length and breadth of the land may receive abundant showers of the Holy Ghost, in answers to the laid-up prayers of our witnessing forefathers. It is encouraging to know that in many places, abroad and at home, God's blessed work is going on still. Glorious work, which has gone on in spite of every opposition for eighteen hundred years, and shall go on till time shall end!

And now, before we close, let us once more entreat you who are unconverted to turn to Jesus. Could ministers but give you some faint idea of Christ's willingness to save you! If any soul here can declare that it is willing to receive Christ, let it know that Christ is yet more willing to save and to bless. He does not wish you to remain an hour longer a stranger to his love. Why did he suffer? Why did he die? Oh! not merely that he might be glorified in your destruction. True, he will yet be so, if you continue to reject and despise him, but that is not what he is seeking now. He did not need to leave his throne in glory to seek that. He need not have left the Father's bosom in order to have the glory of this world's condemnation. He could have got that by leaving the world alone in its sins, and under the curse of God. And for what then, did he leave his Father's bosom, and bleed and die on the cross, but just to be able to say, 'Come unto me, and I will give you rest.' Is no one going to obey that call to-night, and to come, crying, 'Lord, save me, I perish'? Christ is in the offer of every soul in this place, to-night. The Father's unspeakable gift is within the reach of every one now. Blessed be God that a willing people still flee unto him in the day of his power. Jesus *has* a day of power, even in this lost world. He has 'an arm that's full of power.' Believer! can't you set your seal to that? Have you never felt your soul drawn out after him, drawn forcibly—drawn irresistibly—drawn by a power that you have not got, a power that man never exerted, and that angel does not possess? Fellow-sinner, seeking salvation! is the devil whispering in your ear, 'If you are to be saved, you will be saved; and if not, your trying will do no good'? Be sure that God is saying to you, 'Return.' Oh! is no sinner returning to-night? Are none crying out—'Behold we come unto thee, for thou art the LORD, our God'?

6

EVE OF THE DISRUPTION

[*This Address was given by Burns on the evening preceding the Disruption in the church of the Rev. A. Moody Stuart. Just before the Disruption ministers assembled in it to arrange their course for the morrow. At the close of Burns's Address, we observed, in walking past St George's, that the door was open. The Rev. Dr Candlish was about to dissolve one of the Societies connected with his Congregation. As only a few auditors were present, it may be interesting to insert here the last brief and striking words spoken within its walls by the revered minister of St George's.—See pp. 87–90.*]

The woman of Samaria asked our Lord concerning the Jewish worship and her own. From his answer, it is very evident that Christ's great object was to enlighten this woman's mind in the matters which most concerned her. In times when important controversies agitate the land, men are constantly making them a shelter in which to escape from direct personal drawing near to God in Christ. Thus we see, that when the Lord came to close dealing with the soul of this poor woman, she turned off his searching words by asking his judgment on the great controversy of that day. It is much to be feared, that this is just what men are doing in Scotland now. They shift off all inquiry as to the state of their hearts and consciences, into the taking up of a side, and embracing of a principle: and though the side be the Lord's, and though the principle be good, yet it is plain, that if this be all the length to which their religion goes, it cannot save them. It is hard to see them holding fast a truth which condemns, while they let go a truth which might save them. For this truth they contend, that Christ is the King and only Head of his church. But then, that is a truth in the order of God which grows out of this *first* truth, that Christ is the King and the Head of each man who believes. If a man blindly hold the second, and neglect the first; if he contend that Christ reigns in the church, while he has never yet been enthroned in his own heart—the truth he holds will not be silent; no, but it will speak to condemn, it will arise in judgment, and strike him dumb eternally.

Let believers beware of this in days like these; let them plead for a great outpouring of the Spirit of the Lord (as we are this night met to do) upon all the church, and especially upon the body of ministers and elders now assembling. It is easy to perceive that, if these trials, which are at the door, do come, without a great measure of the Spirit along with them, the most fearful consequences will ensue. Where will ministers be who do not receive that, when they lose the influence belonging to their present position? They will either get influence by carnal means (and they are to be pitied who get it in that way), or they must get it by being men evidently full of the Spirit of their Master, and publicly owned by him, as those who are winning many souls to Christ.

But though we must mark the dangers of times like these, and though we must declare that this principle, that Christ is Head of the church, only arises out of the first principle, that Christ is the only Head and lawful Lord of each soul whom he has bought with a price, we dare not neglect this truth for which the Church of Scotland is now contending, and for which all God's faithful people in the land are called to be the witness. Christ did not neglect to set the woman right in her inquiries regarding the true worship: he told her that salvation is of the Jews. Some in the present time say that this truth ought to be kept back, because men will substitute it for the truths regarding their own salvation. My dear friends, we sin and err when we withhold one of God's truths to give place to another; and we dare not call it a secondary truth. This single truth is worth a thousand worlds. It is of more importance than the salvation of all men. It is more precious than all creatures, for it concerns the honour, the crown, the kingdom, and the glorious person of Immanuel, who is Head over all things to the church. Therefore let us hold it fast. But do not make the holding it a test of salvation; many who defend it, are not the Lord's; many who adhere to it, adhere not to the kingdom set up in the heart where Jesus reigns.

Plead for God's ministers who are going forth. Plead that they may be like the company of the early Christians, who were filled with the Spirit, and who went about publishing abroad the gospel of the kingdom. If our ministers were but men full of the Holy Ghost at this time, they would be a light to Scotland, to Britain, and to the world. Scotland could not hold them. Britain could not contain them. The field would be the world. Oh, there is danger, lest the prospect of a settlement in some parish with a few people, should be the means of dragging them down from the position which God has given them. The command is to preach the Gospel to *every creature* in the *whole wide world*. The Lord has given them wonderful light hitherto in the ways of his commandments. Plead for more of this. Plead for humbling to us all, ministers, elders, and people. Plead for this much forgotten and neglected work of God's convincing Spirit, even humbling, because of his hand upon us. If a time of blessing be near at hand, it will be given. O, that our Assembly were like the assembled hundreds of years ago, which was indeed a Bochim, a place of weeping. But where are our tears? How few are gathering into God's bottle. Where are the tears of ministers, preachers, elders, and people?

The following is an extract from the prayer: 'We roll the case of the whole church upon thee. Pour out thy Spirit of grace on thy ministers now assembling in this place. Pour it out upon elders, upon preachers, and upon all holding more private positions in the church. Lord, pour it out upon the students of divinity. Raise up such a race of young men in Scotland, so full of thy Spirit, so devoted to thy service, as shall put all of us to shame, and make us begin to doubt our being born again, and begin to ask whether, indeed, the Lord himself hath given us our commission, to preach the gospel of his Son.'

In closing the meeting in St George's, Dr CANDLISH said, 'I have to request that on the conclusion of this meeting, those who take an interest in the St George's Indian Missionary Association, remain to pass a resolution which the office-bearers of our society have put into my hands. It is to the effect that the St George's Association be this night dissolved. It is evident, brethren, that the dissolution of an Association like this, must remind every one of the winding up, now nigh at hand, of many other similar associations; nay, that it is the immediate forerunner of the breaking up of this congregation in its present connection. It is a thought as solemn as it is difficult to realise, that this night we are on the very eve of an event which is to bring about so many momentous consequences, and the sounding of which will be heard more or less distinctly to the utmost bounds of Christendom, even the event of the disruption of our National Establishment. We can now speak of it as a thing certain, in so far as we can speak of any event not yet past, that to-morrow's sun will behold its goodly structure rent in twain; that before the setting of to-morrow's sun, scenes will be enacted, which will find the Establishment of the country as the company of two armies; and to prevent this, I believe that nothing short of a miracle would be sufficient.

'We are very apt, when living in times like the present, and in circumstances such as those in which this night we stand, very much to underrate and underestimate the magnitude of the results of these events which are passing around us. Unable to grasp a comprehensive view of these in all their extensive bearings, and surrounded and engrossed by the passing and trivial occurrences of ordinary life, such events often produce a far deeper influence on the minds of those who behold them from a distance, than they do upon the men who are themselves the actors in them. Be that as it may, and be our insensibility ever so great, the truth, I believe, is this, that to-morrow will see the spectacle of the consummation of a great revolution in this land, the effects of which, as I before said, will not be experienced in this land alone, a moral and a religious revolution, the greatest that has taken place since 1688, if not the greatest that has taken place since the grand revolution of the Reformation. We are familiarised with hearing such an event spoken of as an everyday occurrence is spoken of; and we almost begin to listen to the recital of what a few years ago were unheard of transactions, with coolness, and sometimes with apathy. But, brethren, I ask not, "How do Scotchmen look on the scenes passing around them?" but I ask, "How do men of other *nations* look upon us?" I do not say in England. England has her faithful ones; but, alas! over her there is come a cloud of awful delusion and heresy. But cross the Channel, or cross the Atlantic, and how do men there look upon us? I speak of the serious, the thoughtful, the religious men of other lands. Brethren, they know the value of these principles for which we contend, and they see that, though not indeed *too* dearly bought, yet we are willing to sacrifice to them our earthly all; and they look on with intense interest to see what will be the end of this momentous struggle. And the eyes of our own countrymen are beginning to open. If they resist not the light, they will soon believe, what the people of the living God have been too slow to learn, that the world and evangelical religion must soon part company. A state of things was coming about in this land, for which no provision is made in the Word of God, and therefore we might have foreseen that it could not last long. Evangelical religion was beginning to be fashionable, at least a profession of it was in no way inconsistent with fashion. It was finding its way, esteemed, unopposed, and sometimes flattered, into the drawing-rooms of the great; and the purest form of the religion of Jesus had begun to be dandled on the lap of this world's ease and favour. Such an order of things could not last long. The law of God forbids that it should be so: the enmity of Satan renders it impossible: and so to rid himself of these obnoxious truths, he usually employs two means, of the practical working of both of which the

British Empire offers abundant proofs. The one method—perhaps the most effectual, and the most like to that which would deceive, if it were possible, the very elect—is that of introducing, through the channels of pure religion, a spurious substitute for it, assuming its appearance, but wholly destitute of its essentials, nay, full of the most soul-destroying delusions, these being the most dangerous, the more imperceptible they are, and the better they are concealed. That is the one weapon used by the great deceiver to destroy the power of the truth. The other is very different in many of its features, for it consists in the open persecution of the woman's seed by the serpent, and through his willing agents upon the earth, and in the raising up of a storm of opposition to the truth when faithfully preached. Both these methods are now employed in these lands; the former in a sister church, the latter in our own country. This war seems to be but beginning. What shall be the end thereof?'

7

THE LORD PASSING BY

[*The following address was delivered in the Free Middle Church, Perth, on the evening of Sabbath, February 12, 1844. It is given as it was delivered; the previous addresses are considerably shortened from the original notes. It is believed that some readers will like to possess one specimen with that redundancy of expression and repetition of the same line of thought, which was customary with Burns, when he did not feel that the first part of his address had told on the consciences and laid hold on the hearts of his audience. Sometimes, on such occasions, when the circumstances did not admit of continuing the service longer than the usual time, he would shut the Bible with a look of sadness, as though he feared that they had met in vain. At other times, he would patiently go over the ground again, in varied words, until those before him were hemmed in and shut up to realise the truth which he declared. That over-awing sense of the Lord's presence, without which he never was satisfied to conclude a service, filled the place or hung over the assembled multitude on the hill side, nor did it depart till sleeping souls had been awakened and had taken the first step on the way to heaven.*]

'I PASSED BY.'—*Ezekiel 16. 6.*

This chapter contains a figurative and wonderfully exact representation of our state as sinners, and also a real representation of the Lord's covenant. The first truth we notice is that contained in the third verse, describing the birth and origin or parentage of those addressed, teaching the great truth that we are depraved, wholly and utterly so, lying under the curse of sin; because, *first, we are cursed in our birth.* The Canaanites were the people of the curse, while the children of Israel were ever made a blessing. This infant, then, was born in Canaan, and its father was an Amorite. Verily this is true; our father has sinned, and in him we have broken the divine covenant, individually and personally, offended the divine majesty, lost the divine image, and entered this world the children of disobedience; not as the children of our Father who created us, but of our father who degraded us. Here God reminds his own people of what they were. This chapter loudly tells us to 'look unto the rock whence we were hewn, and to the hole of the pit whence we were digged.' One look at that will shew us that we were indeed as a child cast out in the day of its birth, lying in all our natural pollution, to the loathing of our person. Ah, brethren! the nature of man is utterly and entirely polluted. The works of the flesh are these, envyings, murders, drunkenness, revellings, and such like; and 'the heart is deceitful above all things and desperately wicked.' Confess now to the Lord and to yourselves, that you are in a state of pollution.

But, *secondly, we are also in a state of rejection.* As an infant thrown away, not pitied, or blessed, or cared for, so is man by nature cast out from the presence of God, and separated from him for ever, his transgressions having brought him into a state of rejection and disgrace, whence none can draw him forth. Again, we are *in a state leading to death*—certainly ending in the ruin of soul and body, should none be found to deliver. The margin expresses it as 'trodden under foot'—cast out, without any to pity, and therefore ready quickly to die.

Such are some of the views which this supposed case gives of the state of man. You see that each of us is by nature under the curse, because he is born of those who are themselves under it, and because, in the person of Adam, their representative, the entire human race has broken the divine covenant, and cast off the allegiance of God, rejecting him as their Father and Head. This is a truth of which the Word of God is full. It is not so much declared as a separate truth, as it is bound up in every other truth.

Men are fond of speculating as to the origin of evil, but no countenance is given to this in the Word of God, where we are simply told that man is depraved; and we see it in Cain, who was born in the image of his father Adam, and of his father the devil. There never was one born among the millions of the world that did not go astray, speaking lies from the beginning. Our mouth is as that of a serpent; we are as a deaf adder, we cannot hear the voice of the living God. See what a view the Lord takes of our state as he sits in the heavens: 'God looked down from heaven upon the children of men, to see if there were any that did understand, that did seek God.' And what report does he give? Ah! how it might lay our pride, for it is the very same he gives to-night of this vast assembly, 'Every one of them is gone back; they are altogether become filthy; there is none that doeth good, no, not one.' This description extends and applies to the youngest and the last of Adam's posterity, to men of every rank, age, and condition. There is not one on whom the traces and marks of the fall are not written and engraved; and if you or I wish to understand the nature of our guilt, look at it as the iniquity of a reasonable being, and the rebellion of a responsible agent.

But, alas, alas! my dear friends, polluted creatures with polluted tastes, and eyes put out by sin, do not and cannot see their pollution. They are oftentimes—and indeed always, except the Lord be striving with them—blind to their degradation. Yes, 'there is a generation that are pure in their own eyes, and yet are not washed from their filthiness.' Still, whether you believe it or not, there is in every heart among us a depth of evil sufficient to pollute and to defile a whole universe.

How does our ungodliness pollute us! What polluted creatures does our pride make us! I believe that pride is the sin which, if possible, is more polluting than any other, and yet it is the one which we are always longest of confessing. Sinner, do you know what a proud heart is? Have you ever discovered that you have one within you? Believe it now. And, then, what a proud people we are taken collectively, how hardened against the fear of the Lord, how we cast off his yoke, and disown his right to reign over us, trampling, if we durst, as it were, on his forehead; setting at nought his counsel, and refusing to hear his reproof. Brethren, we are lost creatures, lying polluted by sin, and deservedly abhorred by the holy God. Yes; and that sin is ours; remember, it is your own, flowing not from outward causes to us, but out from our own hearts; we are lying in our own blood, and that is what makes you and me so vile, so abominable, so loathsome, in his eye, deserving to be cut off and cast out for ever; and yet proud, yet rebellious!

And oh! the helplessness of this state, no man can help us: ministers cannot help us, godly friends cannot help us, parents cannot help their children, the head of the human race could not have helped his descendants, at least except by pointing through himself as a figure to the second Adam, even the Lord from heaven. That was the utmost that by his own example he could do. It is the only way in which any lost sinner can seek to help another, to point to the Lamb of God. We are cast out by man, we are cast out by our first father, by all on earth, into the open field, unhelped, unpitied, friendless, unprotected, lost, and left to be destroyed by that roaring lion, the enemy of souls; and last of all, unable to help ourselves. Poor, helpless, hopeless sinner! this is a faint but fitting emblem chosen by the Divine Spirit to represent your case and mine; for all, all, all are lying in this fearful state.

Blessed be God, a remedy has been found. Not that we mean to say that the evil has been cured. Far be it from us to preach a gospel that is to put all things right in the world, and produce universal quietness, and order, and peace; for however free the gospel offers are—and they have been free to all the world for ages past—multitudes have perished eternally. The gospel offer comes too late to-night for many in your city; thousands have gone from thence to the place of darkness, and are lost beyond recall; and I fear it comes too late for some here, because they will not receive it. What follows, as to the way of salvation, is given in God's own manner, and in his own appointed order. He looks down from his sanctuary's height upon fallen, ruined man, and sees him living in open rebellion against his righteous rule, and in a state of apostasy, resting under the curse; being polluted in his mind as well as his condition by continuance in sin; while no one thing connected with him, except it be his misery and ruin, is fitted to attract the regard or the mercy of the Lord. Nothing is to be seen about him but what is the loathing and the abhorrence of all holy creatures, and, above all, of the Holy One of Israel. The sins of the unrepentant are even objects of loathing to those who are written among the living in Jerusalem, as well as to holy angels.

These, then, are the objects which meet the Lord's eye; and, lo! while you expect to see swift destruction coming forth upon them from his presence, and while you look to see him cast the sinner into hell and to the blackness of darkness for ever, a voice speaks in mercy, and it says in majesty—'I passed by'! The Lord descends from the heavens, and draws near to the poor, lost, outcast, dying sinner, lying still in his 'own blood,' and he saith unto him, LIVE! And oh! it is no empty sound, no merely merciful word of pity, when the Lord says to a sinner, 'Live,' for at the sound his heart has turned to God; he complies with the call of wondrous grace; he turns, he listens, he obeys; at the Lord's reproof, his heart yields, he gives in, while the Lord pours out his free Spirit upon him.

And then, when the soul has been made alive, what follows? 'I spread my skirt over thee, and covered thy nakedness: yea, I sware unto thee, and entered into a covenant with thee, saith the Lord God, and thou becamest mine.' The poor sinner deeply needs such a covering; for, at the same time when God comes thus to give us covering, your soul and mine are naked, having no kind of covering of our own by nature, but needing both to be washed and cleansed from iniquity by the Lord's own hand, and to be clothed from head to foot. Therefore, when Jehovah thus gives life to a dead sinner, he leads him away to the fountain of his dear Son's blood; and once made white and clean for ever there, he clothes the naked soul with the perfect righteousness of his Well-beloved. Nor does he stop there, he makes a full promise for time and eternity, 'I sware unto thee, and entered into a covenant with thee, and thou becamest mine.' In the day in which God calls any sinner, he enters into a covenant with him, and the first thing he engages for, comprehends everything—he engages to be the sinner's *all in all*—'I will be a God unto thee;' and when he says that, does he not indeed say all? For everything is bound up in that— the Lord cannot say more.

But there are two promises which he makes to the soul specially in that solemn, blessed day; the first is, 'Though your sins be as scarlet, they shall be as white as snow;' and the second is, 'I will put my laws into their hearts, and in their minds will I write them.' And then it is that the soul, being quickened and made alive indeed unto God, and *enabled* as well as *inclined* by his power to receive the Lord Jesus Christ, hears in his heart a voice which whispers, 'Thou art mine.' 'I sware unto thee, and entered into a covenant with thee, saith the Lord God, and thou becamest mine.' And oh! the Lord *never* gives up the right that he takes over the soul in that day; come what will, oppose what may, that soul is kept by the Lord, as his own peculiar property, to all eternity.

In order that we may all get a fuller view than I fear we are yet doing, of this, let me call you to fix your minds more particularly upon some of the points, already named, a second time. And first, let me entreat you to consider well the source whence this salvation springs. It is not from the creature, not from man himself, in respect either of merit or power. Merit! how can it be, when all that he ever can appear in God's sight is loathsome and abominable—oh, no! There is truly nothing to attract in poor, fallen man; all that is to be found in him, 'that is, in his flesh,' is opposition to God's law, opposition to his being, opposition to his will, opposition to his glory. Our carnal minds are enmity against God, enmity against his law, enmity to his holy perfections, enmity to his sovereignty.

It is no merit in man that draws forth God's love. What,

think you, could tempt any man to look upon a poor cast-out infant, such as the chapter we are reading describes? What but love could move him? Oh? surely nought but the purest pity and the tenderest compassion would lead a man to take on himself all the care and trouble needful to relieve, to save, and then support the poor and outcast little one.

And it is nothing, nothing but love, unbounded, unmeasured, incomprehensible, it is nothing but divine pity and compassion, it is nothing but the infinite yearnings of an eternal love that moves the holy Lord of heaven to pity *you*. This may well bring down your pride, believers. This may bring down your proud countenance and your high looks, when you think how for many a day, in your nature, in your character, in your conduct, in your heart, in your life, you have been grieving and provoking your Creator and Redeemer; that you have been abominable in his sight—a withered branch, a degenerate vine. Your state has not been a whit less hateful to his sight, nor your sin less heinous, than that which moved him to destroy the old world entirely and for ever; not a whit less heinous in his sight than the sin of the fallen angels who are cast out for ever from his presence—aye, the sin that provoked the thunders of his wrath then, is more hateful in sinners now.

Ye that dwell under the gospel, *one* such call would tenfold increase your guilt above theirs. If you had never heard the gospel, your case were different; but you have heard, and heard for years upon years, until your guilt has become awfully aggravated. Yet, if any are getting a view of their natural pollution, and feeling that by nature they are a *sink* of evil of every kind; that every monster-form of sin that ever grew out of a creature's heart has its seeds and its like in yours; that you never heard of any sin being

committed that has not a counterpart in you, were temptation to blow upon corruption; and that you conceive
hourly sins, more than you have the means of acting out.
Oh! if you are indeed crying to the Lord in words like
these: *I cannot look upon myself; if the Lord's people even
could see my heart they would turn away amazed from me,
and ministers would have nothing to do with me; could any
fellow-sinner see me as I stand in God's sight, he would not
speak to me, how much less the Holy One of Israel!*—take
courage, it is a creature in that very state, in so far at least
as words can describe a lost sinner's state, it is on such—
YES, ON SUCH—that the God of love hath turned his eye,
and to whom, in passing by, he says, LIVE, LIVE.

Do not think that you must make yourself pleasing in
the sight of the Holy One of Israel to be accepted by him.
Fellow-sinner, he knows your state, and he does not make
it better either. It is when in thy blood he speaks to thee.
He repeats it, 'Yea, I said unto thee, when thou wast in
thy blood, LIVE.' These words spring from his own infinite love, from his everlasting, free, unsought mercy,
from the infinite yearnings of a heart of overflowing loving-
kindness. And then observe, he does not wait till you go to
him, till you learn his ways, and love to seek his face. He
would wait long enough if he did; he would wait for ever.

Would any one possessed of reason expect the poor
infant that we are likened to, to rise up and walk, or to
wash and purify itself? Ah no! The benevolent individual
who saves it, feels in this way: If I don't go to it, and go
now, its strength will fail, and its soul will perish. This is
what the Lord sees in each one of us, and so he comes to
the sinner, approaches, as it were, quite close to him, and
whispers in his heart, 'Come, now, and let us reason to-

gether; though your sins be as scarlet, they shall be as white as snow; though they be red like crimson, they shall be as wool.' It is in a marvellously attractive, winning character that the Lord appears at this time. The work is wondrous. It is saving; it is Godlike in the self-moved nature of its origin, in the sovereign freeness and spontaneous bestowal of its gifts. For see, again, the great, the glorious, the holy, the compassionate, the divine Deliverer descends, draws nigh, comes up to where the poor sinner is lying forlorn, cast out, miserable, hopeless, dying, perishing eternally; yea, and polluted, too, and almost dropping into hell, on the very verge of the second death; and Jehovah saith unto him, LIVE.

Ah! sinner, whence is that? What does it mean? It is the coming forth of *eternal compassion*. It is the bursting forth of the waters of divine, unending life! It is the drawing of the cords of everlasting love! It is the gentle yet omnipotent constraint of the bands of the man Christ Jesus! The Lord has come nigh, the Holy Ghost is given, the sinner is saved, and the Saviour is glorified.

Well, you say, and this is all true; but what is that to me? I, who am covered with sins, every one of which deserves eternal fire, each of which makes me a fit subject for the second death, each of which cries for the holy, righteous, and unmingled vengeance of the Lord—what can I do? My dear friend, I allow it, *you can do nothing*! The Lord takes all that into account; yea, he tells you that you do not see half so much guilt in yourself as he sees. Well, but what does he do next? He points you to the fair, white righteousness of the Lord Immanuel, and says, 'Behold the Lamb!' People of God, *you* know well that speaking will not save, and hearing will not save, unless the Lord comes. Prophecy to the breath that it may come upon us in this hour.

Another view which we wish to impress upon you, though we have in part described it already, is, *that the sinner is helpless*. Many think that they can, at their own pleasure, rise and walk. My dear friend, let me ask again, was this poor infant able to rise and walk? Did it even know him who came to save it? Could it thank him? Could it raise its infant wail aloud? Or could it send forth so much as one despairing cry for pity? No, no! And, believe it, could Jehovah descend to this, and promise to give you eternal glory for one motion towards himself, you would be lost. There is nothing between you and perdition but the forbearance of an infinitely holy God. The Lord waits not until the sinner can come to him; he comes up to the sinner. *Are any longing for his presence?* and do you yet feel that your heart is like a stone? The sinner feels that he is chained and bound, and that the devil has him, and will ruin him; and, moreover, that all the creatures in the world cannot save him; and so the Lord, hearing his cry, and seeing his despair, comes near to help him.

Believe this. A heart *less full of tenderness* than his would do the same. You may suppose that if one with like passions to ourselves were passing in any direction, and hearing a faint infant cry, would he not stop? Yes, he turns aside, he pities, and he saves. Faint emblem, that little sufferer, of the case before us; faint is the view it gives of him who comes to save; faint type and shadow of the love that is everlasting. Oh! that you, perishing souls, were looking out to-night for the deliverer! I know you cannot pray to him, as you call it, acceptably. Oh! but he wants you to pray miserably, to pray desolately. He sees in you a returning rebel. You have hated him; you have fought against him; the very heart, and hands, and mouth, and soul, and strength, and youth, or riper years, that are his own gift, and which he created, that with them you might ever love and glorify him, you used against him; and with the very comeliness which he had put upon thee, and with the powers which he hath given thee, hast thou served the devil, drunk up sin greedily, and dishonoured thy God.

Oh, is your heart softening? is it even to him, to this God of salvation, against whom you have sinned, that you would come? Do you look to him? do you cry to him, 'undone, ruined'? The Lord only answers, LIVE. And in this new and eternal life which he begins in you, from first to last he will be honoured, and you will be humbled, while you praise him in an eternal song! Yes, thousands of such vile sinners are now around the throne, making the arches of heaven ring with the praises of the King of saints and the Saviour of sinners. And then the thought, that it is nothing else that attracts the Lord but just this, that 'God is love.' No other account is given but just 'when I passed by thee, and saw thee polluted in thine own blood, I said unto thee when thou wast in thy blood, Live; yea, I said unto thee when thou wast in thy blood, Live.' It may be that the Lord is now passing by. It is not unlikely that he may be saying, Live; for wherever two or three are gathered together in his name, he is in the midst of them. Sinner, are you not afraid lest he pass by you, and pass away without looking upon you? for eternity is at hand, and heaven's gates are barred against the unregenerate. Are you, then, seeking to attract his eye?

People of Perth! the Lord has been saying, 'Live', to many a one in the midst of you. He did so gloriously four years ago, and some of those remain unto this present, and some are fallen asleep. Many of you allowed that season to pass away; you were *afraid* he would say, *Live!* You were *afraid* he would pluck you out of the fire and from a yawning hell, and take you from the devil! Fellow-sinner! He may yet pass you by; for he passes by multitudes, and leaves them to perish; and yet, yet, he has set his heart on a happy few, and saved and blessed them. He has been passing through Scotland for more than three years *evidently*, and the crown is flourishing upon his head yet; in our beloved land, our new churches tell *that*, and testify that he is the Lord of all. Oh, then, brethren! will you not submit yourselves to him? Perhaps you are sitting in some quiet corner, and conscious that you are one of whom nobody is thinking; and it may be so; but Jesus is thinking of you; will you not say to him, 'Save, Lord, I perish.' The poor world knows it not, sees not that he is passing by; but will *you* not look to him? He sees you in your blood, sees you to be vile, and black, and ungodly; so vile that perhaps the people of God—some of them— would not like to have much to do with you.

Is there one such among you? Let us trace his feelings. He first begins to say, *Where is God?* and then the truth is awfully revealed to him that it is no delusion; that there is a God in the earth; and when he hears that God saying to him, LIVE, he cannot believe it. Still the sinner is drawn, and begins to think again. Young men, are there any of you who stop here, and cannot say even that there is a God? It is a great point gained when a man can do that from the heart. Oh! that ministers came into the pulpit in the strength of that belief, something would breathe around them that would shake the infidelity of others. It is a blessing when this great truth is set up; for then the sinner begins to bend to the authority of the Word of God, and feels that his throne may shake before one jot or tittle of that Word will fall away. Many a hard battle he will have with the devil before this be granted; many a fall and many a blow from Apollyon's sword. But then the love of the Lord Jesus comes in here; and, dear fellow-sinners, if there be one present in such affecting circumstances, that love *will* draw you from Satan's power. You say, 'I am unclean,' and so you are; but he will put you into the fountain opened for sin and for uncleanness; and if you tell him that your sins are 'red like crimson,' he will shew you that the blood of his cross cleanseth from sin of every dye. And then, if you doubt again of the sufficiency of the sacrifice, or of Immanuel's ability to save, he will shew you that he who was the Man of sorrows, is the Man who is Jehovah's fellow too, and thus he will answer every question, and remove your every doubt. What but the spreading forth of these glorious truths was the means of the Reformation? And what will be the means of converting a single soul, but just the same truth, that Christ hath died to save sinners?

There are many who would stop short of this, and yet who like to come to get their feelings moved, Sabbath after Sabbath; while week after week finds them back again at their worldliness and mammon worship. They always take care that the truth will never reach so deep into the heart as that the citadel shall be taken. Oh! that you would now simply say, 'Lord, I perish, save thou me.' When that cry ascends, an answer comes; and, ah, then there is a bond formed, which neither time, nor death, nor hell, can ever rend: and when he ties the eternal knot, believe it, nor death nor hell can break it. 'Who shall separate us from the love of Christ?' What! shall persecution? No, persecuted

believer, even you may raise the song, 'Who shall separate?'
For why? Will not the Lord save and guard his own truth?
The saints may be imprisoned, ministers silenced or
banished, God's people may be *hung up* for the truth's
sake, but the truth itself will not be hung up or stifled. No,
it will spread, it will run, it will be glorified in times like
these. The truth of Christ, and the saints' union to him,
will bloom on the gibbet, and spring up into beauty and
renown from their open graves. What! think you they will
bind Immanuel's truth? Will they fetter his love? Will
they limit his glorious sovereign grace? Will they draw a
bolt before the great Breaker? Ah, no! He hath opened the
two-leaved gates, and now devils, and death, and tribula-
tions, are like captives at his chariot wheels. The Breaker is
ascended on high; he is on the throne now, and if any of
you are receiving him into your hearts, you will soon get
the reward of his chosen; you will have your feet on the
neck of the old serpent soon. Oh! then, now, when he is
passing by, will you not quickly join yourselves unto him?
Our time for repentance will soon be over; all our meetings
will soon be over; and when *the great meeting* comes, and
when we stand face to face in the presence of the Lord,
and all you have ever heard comes fresh into your memory,
what will be the feelings of many a gospel hearer then?

Observe, it was not the crowds that attracted the notice
of the Lord on the day when he passed through Jericho;
the individual who got good from him was a poor blind
man. Fellow-sinners, *you* have no knowledge of who is this
night present to bless us. It is Jesus of Nazareth. *You*
have never discovered him, but this blind man did.
Bartimaeus had heard of him, and, doubtless, said within
himself, 'Well, if I lose this opportunity, I may never have

another; I can't see him, I can't go to him, but I'll cry.' And so he did cry, 'Jesus, thou Son of David, have mercy on me.' The disciples did not like this, it was against their ideas of the Lord's dignity. The procession was too fine to be disturbed by the cries of a beggar.

And how much like this is the present state of things! Our congregations are in too good order to be troubled by anxious souls! Propriety would not allow it! Oh, my dear friends, if you begin to seek the Lord, many will cast cold water upon your anxiety. They will say, 'What! are you going to be serious?' For I believe that there are multitudes who would rather see their friends going on to the brink of the precipice of perdition, than seeing them becoming grave, and solemn, and heavenly-minded, condemning a careless world by their holy words and lives. Better that an anxious soul should meet with enemies than with cold-hearted professors who are full of the spirit of the world. Let all such precious, and it may be, hidden ones, look much to the High Priest who sitteth in the heavens. This will please him better than anything. If any poor sinner is saying, 'Jesus, thou Son of David, have mercy on me,' he will hear that cry. He did not attend to the crowd that followed him. He stood still. Ah! this is what he does at all times. He *waits* to hear the cry of the penitent. Call upon him; do it secretly; he knows what you are thinking, and he says, 'What wilt thou that I do unto thee?' Bartimaeus said, 'Lord, that I may receive my sight.' Oh, that you would offer up this prayer, and then, not only would you receive your sight, but you would receive pardon, you would receive justification, and indwelling of the Holy Ghost, deliverance from the world, deliverance from Satan's yoke.

Take another instance: remember the poor woman who,

though diseased, went to him in the press. She did not hesitate. She was bold. She knew her necessities, and she knew his ability to save. And, oh, if you would follow her example, you would be, like this woman, immediately healed. For the Lord said, 'Who hath touched me?' Peter said, 'The people throng thee, and askest thou, Who touched me?' The Lord took no notice whatever of this interruption, but went on, 'I perceive that some one has touched me, because virtue has gone out of me.' Oh, brethren, can he say at this moment, 'Somebody hath touched me?' Is there any one who is hardly able, for the crowd, to get within hearing of the Word, who is in some quiet place crying out to the Lord? Then virtue is going out from him; that sinner is saved. Let me be that woman, that man, that child, rather than the wisest or the greatest of this world's children. Many will sit for hours listening to the preaching of the Word; they will never complain of being 'kept in,' as others would call it, and yet they refuse to spend five minutes *alone with Christ*. Ah, brother, will you not begin to do this? it is being alone with God that is the beginning of salvation to many; that is what the devil is afraid of; the last place he likes a sinner to go to is his own quiet room, entering in there when none observes, putting in the bolt with a look that shews you are one who has *something real to transact there*, that you have something to do with God. Ah! Satan well knows that in many cases there is virtue going out of Immanuel then. *Then!* did I say? Oh, there is virtue going *always* out of him; fulness of grace dwells in him.

That fulness is going out at this hour to the poor Hindoos, to the Chinese, the South Sea Islanders, the Kaffirs, and the Hottentots, and among the darkened thousands on our Continent. Oh, yes, in these last days of ours, he is drawing all men unto him. His own ancient people, his beloved Israel, are beginning to look after him; and some few of them are seeing in him the promised King of Zion. People of Scotland! where is the Lord who hath been so honoured in this land in days gone by! Have his martyrs not foretold of days of his right hand to come? 'The covenants, the covenants will yet be Scotland's reviving!'

Blessed be God, such reviving is not wholly gone from the midst of us. Ah, no! There are green spots yet where his dew descends. Do none of you know this? Don't some of you know what it is to have a fireside that is made happy by faces on which the light of his countenance shines? And how sweet at night to hear the melody of joy and health, and the song of praise, when other sounds are hushed. These families are like a little heaven below. Oh, picture of heaven, indeed, when the voices of parents and children blend in praising the Shepherd of Israel and the King of Zion, when all is love, and peace, and kindness, and not a jarring word is heard, nor an angry look is given. What a blessing such a sight might bring to the stranger that beholds it! I shall suppose some such one coming to take up his abode in such a family, it might be, even for a single night; he marks it all, and feels the beauty of it, and says, 'Well, I wish I could be longer there;' or, perhaps, he says to himself as he departs, 'I love that holy joy; I will go and put their religion to the trial', and there, perhaps, begins the return of that wanderer to the fold.

Will none here, in like manner, bethink himself? Do you really believe, my dear friend, that God lives? You know that many people, without being professed infidels, do not in the least believe the children of God, when they say that there is such a thing as going away to be alone with

God, making a request according to the will of God, and getting an answer to their prayer. They think that any idea of that kind is produced by the friction of mere feeling upon the heart; that it is an empty delusion or imagination. Well, but suppose one of you gets a step further than this daring infidelity, and the question is seriously agitated, within you, whether God *is* or *is not*. This is the hour, it may be, of your first real prayer; you go away into a secret place, whether in your dwelling or in the open field, it matters not; and your first impression is, *there is a God, and I will call to him*. Satan says immediately, assuming, as it were, the garb of prudence or of common sense, 'What! whom are you speaking to? Nobody hears you, you are speaking to the air!' And then your own evil heart rises up and joins with him. Many a man thinks he believes in God, just because his faith is so purely nominal that Satan has never thought it worth disputing. His are prayers that never go higher than the back of the chair he kneels at. But, ah! if he took courage and, resolving to get at the truth, went away to pray, a thousand voices would cry within him, There is no God, no God! And some would give up the search here, and swallow the devil's lie, and be ruined eternally. But then, some would not do this, the awakened sinner would not be so easily put off. He feels, as it were, that there is something at the other end of the line that he is casting upwards, and he will not let go his hold. And then, perhaps, he remembers something about that Word of truth, which is called the lamp of the wanderer's foot, and so he opens his Bible. Here again, Satan will perhaps meet him, and will likely whisper, 'I am sure you have read that book all your life long and never got any good by it; it never then can be the Word of God.' Ah! but, my dear friends, Satan's lie won't pass so easily now that he has been proved a liar; and being resisted, he will perhaps flee. So the man goes on; some word of promise meets him, and, as he reads, he comes to more; and there another light has risen to cheer him onwards, till he finds in Immanuel matchless fulness for his every need. And then he joins himself to the Lord's dear people too, and unites with them in the work and labour of love, which they have to finish ere the 'night,' which is at hand, 'cometh,' and ere they hear the knock of the Judge who standeth before the door.

Oh, are you all 'watching unto prayer,' beloved? I think some at least, are surely doing this. I am sure there were some who rose early this morning, perhaps 'a great while before day,' to plead with the Captain of the Lord's host that he would come forth this day in the midst of us, 'conquering and to conquer.' *Persevere*, beloved in the Lord, 'in due time ye shall reap if ye faint not.'

We would entreat every one of you to imitate the example of those who went round the city of Jericho. They were to compass it seven times; once would have done as well had the Lord appointed it so, but he teaches his people perseverance by these means; and then, at last, when Jericho did fall, what was the occasion of it? Nothing but the blowing of trumpets of rams' horns—a weak breath. Oh, how the foolishness of man is used to work the purposes of the Lord! In the same way can he make a single sentence, pronounced by a little child, effect what no persuasion or eloquence could accomplish. When the wall of Jerusalem was to be rebuilt, every man went and builded opposite his own house. You that are a husband, begin this night; when you go home, speak to your wife tenderly and solemnly; beseech her to begin to consider 'the things that belong to her peace,' and do not give up for one refusal. I confess that I often feel tempted to do this. I often say, 'I'll give up preaching, why continue it?' And so, when you go home, you may be tempted to say, 'It's all very well for the minister to tell me to speak to my household, but it is useless to attempt it.' My dear friend, remember the blowing of the rams' horns. And let another take a servant apart, and the brother his sister.

When the Lord does give the word, great is the company of them who publish it. Every one will then speak to his neighbour, and the friend to his friend; or you, dear children, to your companions at school. Why not begin at once to seek to convince them and lead them to Jesus, imploring the Lord your Shepherd to work by you. He can do much by the testimony of a little child, saying simply what it knows of the evil of its heart, and of the faithfulness of Jesus. Such a testimony makes those around begin to inquire, What am I? Am I saved? What ground have I to hope if these things are true?

The moment a man trusts God's promise, he is a child of God. The moment he takes the Lord at his word, and believes his testimony concerning his Son, that moment he is safe. I remember being struck with an anecdote told of Napoleon Bonaparte's review of his troops.—In passing, we might ask, Where are Bonaparte and his armies now? So passes the glory of the world!—During the review, the emperor's horse became restive; in trying to quiet him, his hat fell off; a young *lieutenant* happened to pick it up, and when he restored it, Bonaparte said, 'Thank you, *captain.*' The young man took advantage of the word, and immediately said, 'In what regiment, sire?' 'The Guards,' answered Napoleon. The young man did not wait; he went and took his place. The other officers said, 'What right have you here?' He said, 'I am a captain of the corps.'

'What, who made you that? Where is your uniform?' Ah! he had *the emperor's word*, and he wanted and needed no more. Brethren, imitate this little incident in the more solemn matter of your soul's salvation. Are you a sinner? Are you in the ranks of the condemned, fallen men of this world? Oh! do you hear the Lord's voice telling you that you may be saved, and saying, 'I will be a Father unto thee, and thou shalt be my son' or daughter? Do you doubt him? Will you not answer, 'Surely thou art our Father?' Do not raise questions; do not ask disbelievingly, What will be done with my evil heart? Leave all that to him, and go quickly, go confidently, yes, rejoicing go, and take your place among his children, and your portion with his people, and be to him a son, and be sealed after that ye have believed, with the Holy Spirit of promise, which is the earnest of the inheritance, the first-fruits of the purchase of that glorious possession reserved for you in the heavens.

8

TRUE ZEAL

[*In February 1844, Burns visited Perth for ten days, at the earnest request of those who longed to see an ingathering of souls. Besides three services on the Sabbaths, he had a service every evening, as also at 9.15 a.m., for working people, during their breakfast hour. Prayer for a blessing on the town was followed by a short address to Christians on the way to work acceptably for Christ. Snow was on the ground most of the time, but it did not prevent a large attendance.*]

'BUT IT IS GOOD TO BE ZEALOUSLY AFFECTED ALWAYS IN A GOOD THING.'—*Galatians 4. 18.*

There is nothing more precious than true zeal in the things of God, and nothing, perhaps, which has so many counterfeits. Genuine zeal is simply a soul-absorbing concern for the Lord's glory, and it is thus the highest of all graces: it can only be in lively exercise when love to God is felt, and, indeed, not always then, for it requires a high degree of heart-devotion and self-dedication to put it forth and sustain it. There may easily be a great deal of zeal in a bad cause; so high may that zeal rise, that the true zeal of God's children can scarce keep pace with it. They seldom rival the zeal that will 'compass sea and land to make one proselyte.' There may also be a great deal of bad zeal in a good cause. Alas! that this should be, at all times, so common in the church of God. True zeal is, then, as

113

rare as it is precious; it is a fruit seldom seen among us. Few men are filled with such a desire after God's glory as Christ had, when he said, 'The zeal of thine house hath eaten me up,' or if they do at times feel something approaching to it, it soon evaporates, it does not last. And why is this? Why do those, who were once the most zealous in the work of God, begin to fall asleep? Why do those who used to weep tears of sorrow and pity over the unawakened, and who could not let one act, dishonouring to God, pass unreproved, or at least unmourned, now begin to sit down with careless professors, giving all up in despondency and hopelessness, and even saying in God-dishonouring unbelief, 'We must take things as they are, and leave others to take their own way, and wait God's time?' My dear friends, whoever says *that*, is guilty of treason against the King of kings; and, moreover, whoever *perseveres* in saying that, will bring, ere long, a blight upon his own soul, and it may be, upon all his labours. It is a dangerous thing to cease from the work of seeking to gain others over to the service of our Master; the soul's prosperity is so intimately connected with it, that we cannot neglect it without losing the blessing of God.

On the other hand, if we *are* engaged in a good work, we cannot throw too much energy into it; it is impossible to cast too fervent a heat into genuine heaven-born zeal; for when will our zeal be worthy the followers of the Lord Jesus, who left his throne, and suffered, and bled, and died on this earth, just that he might bring glory to the divine law, and sanctify the Father's name, in the redemption of lost sinners, by the blood of his cross?

'It is good to be zealously affected always in a good thing.' And were none of you ever thus affected? Some of you *were* zealous in days past. Has it lasted? Examine yourselves as to this, while we mention one or two things which are inseparable from true zeal, and without which it cannot burn with a pure and steady flame.

The first of these, is a *strong spiritual appetite.* A living believer seeks to have an equal relish for all the food which he finds in the Word of God. There is no truth, provided it have Divine sanction, from which he will not extract saving benefit, and life to his soul: the *smallest* parts of God's truth, as we might be apt to call them, have deep attractions in his eyes, and the *plainest* parts of the Word have more charms for him than the most adorned human compositions. Have you this characteristic of a child of God?

The second thing which we shall mention, is *spiritual activity.* This is the first outward manifestation of the existence of true zeal in the heart, and it springs immediately from the spiritual appetite of which we have spoken.

The want of food incapacitates a man from working; unless his body receive due support, he cannot work either hard or long; and so in the divine life, if a man cease personally to live *on* Christ, he cannot work long for Christ among others. Impossible! He may keep up the appearance of this life long after the reality of it is gone: I believe that some now present can confirm the truth of this by painful experience. Are there not some among you who used to warn your fellow-sinners, and pray with them, and employ every means in your power to lead them to Jesus, speaking to them out of a full heart, and with all the earnestness of love?—but now, your efforts are feeble, and what you say is forced, and only said from a sense of duty.

You complain that it does not impress the hearts of

those to whom it is addressed. My dear friend, *it does not pierce your own conscience;* and it is only when a deep and powerful impression of the truth abides on a man's own heart that the word has power to convince and to convert others. Sometimes the words spoken, whether of warning, or in commendation of Christ, are like nothing but dry skeletons of skin and bone, without either life or soul in them, and falling cold and powerless on the ear. But when truth is vividly impressed on the speaker's inmost soul, each word seems to have a volume in it, and every remark drops down sweetness and fresh fragrance.

And why should it not be always thus? Is the glory of Christ not what it once was? Are the interests of God's kingdom less dear to you, or is it so far advanced in the world, that you have nothing now to do but to sit still, and look idly on? Is the state of sinners less awful, or their danger less imminent, because they are so many years nearer eternity? No, brethren. It is we who have changed; it is we who have fallen asleep. Oh! confess it—it is we who are shutting our eyes and folding our hands, and falling asleep over the work, in which our heart and hand, our body, soul, and spirit, our time, talents, life, all, *all* should be engaged. That is not the spirit of the Lord's true people. That is not like the character of your God and Father, or of your Elder Brother in the heavens, for he is a High Priest *for ever*—He intercedeth *ever*—He loveth to the end, and beyond the end of time, even for evermore.

How inconsistent, then, are we, professing as we do to be his chosen people, and to be seeking after conformity to his likeness! You know it is said in one place, that 'all people will walk every one in the name of his god;' even the poor blinded heathen spend much of their strength and substance in the worship of their gods, which 'are yet no gods, but dumb idols.' What! and shall not we then 'walk in the name of the Lord our God for ever and ever?' seeing that he lives and reigns 'the same yesterday, to-day, and for ever.' His glorious power is not less now than it was when first we trusted in him; his long-suffering is not less patient, nor his covenant less secure—his love is not yet removed from us, and his faithful word abideth ever. We have the same Bible we had then; no promise has been taken out of it; the same throne of grace to go to, the same Spirit to help infirmity and strengthen faith. The Son of God is not asleep. Oh, no! He has been interceding for us on high amid all our forgetfulness, barrenness, and indifference. 'Behold, he that keepeth Israel shall neither slumber nor sleep.' But for that, we had been cut down long ago. In his name, then, go forward; forward to do his will.

To some of you we say, Go *forward rather than pray*. Think not that we would, as these words might imply, cast discredit on prayer; but, beloved, our hearts are deceitful, and although we should at every moment have an upward eye and a thirsting heart for the guidance and the presence of the living God, still there are times and circumstances when it becomes almost a sin to pray; sometimes it is unbelief that makes us pray, or rather *seem* to pray—else what does that word mean, 'Why criest thou unto me? speak unto the children of Israel that they go forward.' This shows us that men may, and do, sometimes, slink away from self-denying, disagreeable duties, and go to prayer, when they ought rather to be turning 'the battle to the gate.' You will generally find that these are the times when you will be least able to pray. It were absurd to call true prayer sinful; prayer is our strength, the safeguard of the soul: the Lord the Spirit gives the heart to pray. But let us keep all things in the order which God has laid them, remembering for our encouragement that nothing is ever undertaken for the promotion of the cause of God in which he will refuse to aid us. I would make no exceptions or limitations to this; for I believe that no man, however poor, and weak, and humble, ever did undertake anything with a single heart and eye to God's glory, and according to his will, without finding God in his path, strengthening and supporting him, if not visibly working with and for him.

Believer! can you contradict this assertion? Can you point to the time when you sought, with a sincere and willing heart, to serve and glorify him, and say, that *then* you found him to be a wilderness, or a land of darkness? I know you cannot.

If you desire the continuance of real, solid, spiritual comfort, seek to work diligently for God. You know that mere feeling cannot last long— much of it must necessarily pass away; it lasts for a time, but the mind wears out, and sinks into a cold relapse, and fresh excitement is required to arouse it again. Ah! but that is not like the calm, pure, spiritual feeling, produced by an impression on the will, through the Holy Ghost, elevating the conceptions, purifying the desires, constraining and keeping in subjection the whole heart and mind to the obedience of Christ.

Another mark of zeal, is *implicit, immediate, child-like obedience*. How simple is the obedience of a little child; it does not ask a reason, or form a precise opinion of each step it takes, but readily follows its parent wherever he leads. A calm, unmurmuring obedience is what the Lord seeks from his people, a chastened temper, a renewed will; for such a work in the soul is permanent and abiding, and sends forth a constant flow of holy zeal.

The world will not believe in any real zeal among God's children; the world thinks it is only a natural thing, arising from natural sources, and, therefore, that it will soon wear out and pass off. Alas, that we should give them so much reason to think so! Beloved friends, look at Paul. Did his zeal wear out? Did it diminish? Did the coldness of the prison chill it? Was it broken under the lash? Was it bound by the chains that lay on his body? Did it suffer shipwreck, when he was three days in the depths of the sea? Did the flame of persecution consume it? Did the roaring of wild beasts terrify him out of his zeal for the cross? No; for Christ was revealed within him, and that was a permanent thing.

As men advance in the divine life, zeal becomes purer; it has less of natural emotion in it, and more of God's grace. And, my dear friends, whenever a Christian begins to languish and fall away, the first flower that the wind of temptation nips, is zeal. Pray, then, for us, and for yourselves, that we may endure, shall I say, for a *little* longer—a few years—or *many* years? No; it is *to the end* that we must endure. This is not the language of our own hearts, the flesh is always crying out, 'Stop now, stop now!' Yes, and that is a very comfortable sound in a man's ears, when he is worn out and weary; ay, and a man might begin to think about obeying it, if another voice did not contradict the lie; if God did not say, 'He that shall endure *to the end*, the same shall be saved.' Alas! brethren, we know too well what decays of zeal are; and now that, in the gracious providence of God, we are permitted again to meet in this place, to labour together for the in-gathering of souls, may it be to act boldly, and to enter in, by the open door of Immanuel's glorious and everlasting righteousness, to obtain the promise of the Father,—the great Breaker himself going before us, and Jehovah at the head of us. He breaks up the way for all his children, not only to deliver them from the wrath to come, and from a state of condemnation, but going before them also in all that is undertaken for his glory, and in his name. He does a part of all his works on earth by his people, and enables them to overcome all difficulties, and to overthrow them in the name of the Lord. He makes the worm Jacob, a new sharp threshing instrument, by him beating the mountains as chaff. 'Fear thou not, for I am with thee; be not dismayed, for I am thy God.'

9

UZZA SMITTEN

[Perth, February 1844.]

'AND THE ANGER OF THE LORD WAS KINDLED AGAINST UZZA, AND
HE SMOTE HIM, BECAUSE HE PUT HIS HAND TO THE ARK: AND THERE
HE DIED BEFORE GOD.'—*1 Chron. 13. 10.*

The ark was a type of Christ, and the bringing up of the
ark, at the command of King David, is, in like manner, a
type of the endeavours after the advancement of Christ's
kingdom. David was commanded and authorised to bring
up the ark; he did it not without considering whether it
were pleasing to the Lord, and to his people, and it was,
doubtless, a good desire in him. But then, such good desires
are many times mingled and accompanied with much sin:
and we have an example of this here. David himself had
apparently ordered all things concerning it; we find him
gathering together all Israel, going himself among them,
playing before the Lord, while the ark followed, placed in
a new cart drawn by oxen, under the care of Uzza and
Ahio. All of a sudden the oxen stumbled, and Uzza, in
eager zeal, put forth his hand to keep the ark from falling.
He seemed to be doing right; he was afraid that some evil
would happen to it, and therefore made what would seem
to us a harmless movement, or even one worthy of the
praise and approval of God; but it was not accepted, and

Uzza was put to death for it. What may this not teach us concerning the jealousy of the Lord of hosts when his glory is concerned!

It is not enough to be anxious for the coming of his kingdom. Uzza was anxious to save the ark from falling; but then he touched it not after the due order. We may, then, well tremble at being engaged in the work of the Lord; for zeal, if not according to knowledge, may bring us into rash contact with God's glory, and that will bring us into contact with judgment too, if we work not according to the due order. 'The anger of the Lord was kindled against Uzza, and God smote him there for his error; and there he died by the ark of God. And David was afraid of the Lord that day, and said, How shall the ark of the Lord come to me?'

From this, we learn that there are times when nothing but the lighting down of the Lord's arm will do to cast us down, to chastise and humble us; times when we need to get our accursed pride brought low to the very dust. How wonderful that we should long escape this breaking forth of his power; if it should come, let us take it meekly at his hand, and learn from it the glorious holiness and jealousy of that God who will not be worshipped but after the due order.

But when the ark was thus carried aside, the Lord allowed not the resting-place of his glory to be brought into contempt; he blessed the house of Obed-edom, and all that he had. This seems an emblem of what often happens now; when we are zealously engaged in his work, and meet therein with some heavy rebuke from God, we are terrified and stop, and do not dare to touch it with our hands any more. Well, and does the work of God cease for that? Not so! Whether we will do it or not, whether we take a personal part in it or hold back, or even if we sit down and say that the Lord will not work any more—oh! we hear, all of a sudden, that the ark has appeared elsewhere, and that some other house than ours is blessed because of it. It is a dangerous thing in one sense to be engaged in the work of the Lord—it will lead to chastisement on account of unholy and carnal zeal! but it is equally dangerous to cease from it, for if we do, we shall lose the blessing, and perhaps not find out that we have lost it, till we see it passing us by, and lighting down upon others.

When David saw what a blessed man Obed-edom had become, he was provoked, it would seem, to jealousy in the good work, and made arrangements for carrying it on anew. And so we shall ever find, that when visible, humbling judgments come upon us, they lay us low at the time, and then the Lord's hand again returns to lift us up in Christ Jesus. If there is to be much of the Lord's presence among us as a church, we shall see far more of this than is expected by many who think they are longing for God's work to begin. There would, in that case, be breaches made upon us; visible judgments on the unconverted, visible judgments on believers and on congregations; and these things may be sent for many just causes, both on ministers and people; because, alas! there is much building with untempered mortar.

And were the Lord, indeed, thus to begin to work amongst us, how many would be finding out, that they had come into the ministry, and come into the eldership, and into the deacon's office, and to the communion table, *without a divine call*. And those who feel that they have a divine call, would be finding out, too, that judgments were coming upon *them*, because they had been taking liberties with the work of God. All would be discovering that he is not One whose ways or thoughts are as ours; but that he is a jealous God, who will not give his glory to another, nor his praise to graven images. And yet, remember that if we, out of fear, refuse to go along with the ark, we shall get no blessing.

Let us follow him who is the Angel of the Covenant, seeking to know well whom it is that we follow; not hastily rushing, like Uzza, of our own choice, to this or that other part of his work. Let us go where Jehovah leads; let us pray; let us tremble to offend in the least matter him with whom the blessing lies. Let us seek to be continually engaged in his work, in his way, keeping in mind that we can do nothing, attempt nothing, except as he directs; and even then must it be with constant holy fear and watchfulness, lest a breach be made upon us. Yet this spirit of holy fear is almost unknown among us. Why so? Because there is so little appearance of the Lord's working. More of this would bring more of holy fear, especially upon us in the ministry. One would think, from the way in which God's service is undertaken and performed, that it was a thing any man could do whenever he pleased, instead of being a thing high above us, requiring the constant aid and direction of his Holy Spirit.

But, secondly, we see from this chapter who it was that should carry the ark. A great number of priests were chosen and appointed by God's direction, through David, to this office, and set apart solemnly for it. And in like manner, there is in the church of Christ a race set apart to do service to him, and to carry his gospel through the world—even a royal priesthood. It consists of every true minister of the Lord Jesus Christ. Nor is the work confined to ministers and elders. It is delivered by the Lord into the hands of the New Testament priesthood. We are thus taught that it is the bounden duty of all believers to join in this work, and also warned of the danger of admitting any into it who are not God's people, since they alone will be accepted in it. Alas! this is too often done, others are called in, and the Lord's blessing is withheld.

Their names are given here, and for many reasons, though some may be wearied by such long catalogues. One of these reasons, doubtless, is to shew what a distinction it is in the eyes of the Holy One, to be employed in his service; and not only does this apply to those in the ministry, but to all who are in any way connected with his cause; for they all have this high honour from himself, as well as a heavy responsibility laid upon them.

10

RETURN OF THE ARK

[Perth, February 1844.]

1 Chronicles 15.

All the priests chosen to bring up the ark to the city of David were commanded to sanctify themselves. 'For,' said David to the priests, 'because ye did it not at the first, the Lord our God made a breach upon us, for that we sought him not after the due order.' Experience had taught David; sad when it does not teach us, yet seldom does it teach presumptuous men. David had got the sanctified use of the breaking forth of God's anger upon Uzza. We find also in this account of the ark's return, that many persons were appointed to the giving of thanks. Surely the approach of the King of saints ought to be welcomed by the highest praises of all creatures; yet how cold and lifeless are we in this matter! All the details here given set forth typically the variety of the praises which the children of God owe to him for his varied dealings towards each. And there is a great variety in these. Some can tell of dealings which others cannot comprehend; and, oh! what some souls have to praise him for! How loud will be their song to him who liveth for ever and ever! What notes some will reach! How high their strains!

The form of praise was not left to chance. David delivered the psalm to Asaph with his own hand. It was the spontaneous effusion of that hour, directed by the sending forth of the Holy Ghost, and thus David was full of joy as he approached the resting-place of the ark. He was clothed in a robe of fine linen, which is emblematical of the glorified state of Christ's church, for she is clothed as in fine linen, clean and white, which is the righteousness of saints. And, then, filled with the Spirit, he came forth leaping for joy. This is a state in which the Lord's people can get and need expect no sympathy from the world. None but those who have some acquaintance with the Lord, the source of all their gladness, will be able to bear their company when they are in a very lively state, and enabled greatly to rejoice in the Lord. At such times, the world, like Michal, looks down upon them, and is filled with pity and even hatred towards them.

Michal felt, no doubt, the greatest respect for David in general; she would, no doubt, idolise him, with the thousands of Israel, when the cry was that he had slain his tens of thousands. But when David was more than usually exalted in the Lord and in the power of his might, when he could rejoice in Jehovah all the day, and boast in the God of his salvation—the man after God's own heart—it was then that Michal (who does not appear to have been a godly woman, but one with whom David was unequally yoked, being an unbeliever) saw King David dancing and playing; and she despised him in her heart. Oh! how like to what we see now-a-days, and to what has been and will be seen in every age to exist in the hearts of the unregenerate. How perfectly does it express the contempt of the world towards the godly, not at all times, observe, nor indeed at any time, but just when believers are lifted up in

soul, and enabled to behold him 'whom their soul loveth.'
There is the point at which the enmity of the world begins.

And just as it was not a stranger who mocked David, but
Michal, his own wife, so in families we find that this enmity burns hottest of all. This is often quite imperceptible
in times of deadness, but not when the Lord appears.
Instead of the coming up of the ark into a place, or a congregation, or a family, being a signal for peace, and a cause
of union, it is the very reverse. When the ark of the
covenant comes up and rests among us (should that
blessed and longed-for day ever come) we shall hear of
more disunion yet. Union among believers will grow and
be strengthened and increase; but disunion from un-
believers will increase in proportion. So it is with iron
put into a furnace. Some one might put it in, with all the
clay about it, to harden it and make the substances unite.
But this would not be the case. All the metallic part would
flow together, and become pure and hardened, but the
rest would consume and separate. And where the Lord
appears in his glory, congregations are broken up, and
churches rent asunder; multitudes are seen standing
back in alarm, and none are united but the Lord's true
people, while *they* are despised by relatives and acquaintances, those nearest them in the family or in the church
despising them most.

How little have we of his presence now! The want of
chastisement is one mark of his absence. Were he among
us, there would be more strokes coming direct from the
Lord's hand. There would also be blessings coming direct
from his hand upon all; and his own people would be filled
with the Spirit, devoted to his glory, triumphing in his
praise, and separate from the world. Such a sight as that

would quickly bring reproach, mockery, and suffering in its train.

How did David answer the taunt of his wife? 'It was before the Lord, which chose me before thy father, and before all his house, to appoint me ruler over the people of the Lord, over Israel: therefore will I play before the Lord. And I will yet be more vile than thus, and will be base in mine own sight; and of the maid-servants which thou hast spoken of, of them shall I be had in honour.' Oh, how beautiful! Few, few have such grace!

Look at the psalm which David composed on the occasion of the coming up of the ark. He was not deterred by contempt or ridicule from going on in the praise of the Lord. 'Give thanks unto the Lord. . . . Be ye mindful always of his covenant,' going on to shew how the Lord had been faithful, always rebuking their enemies; working, as now he does, wonderful deliverances for his people, when they do not know it; following them from nation to nation; and many times when they think they are deserted by him, and given over into the hands of their enemies, he is staying the arm of persecution, and saying to their oppressors, 'Touch not mine anointed, and do my prophets no harm,' while he is reproving kings for their sakes. And thus, he leads them by his providence, and protects them by his power, till he brings them to his presence in his house above.

If it be so, let his people be continually remembering their Lord, and declaring his goodness to others. Think of the blessedness of being his people. And when you see houses among you where the Lord seems to dwell, should not such sights incite you to strive to get near him who blesses them and theirs. Remember, that all are not alike in this matter. There is much left to man's free-will. The hand of the diligent maketh rich in the things of God, as well as in temporal mercies. Let the Lord's people resolve, in his strength, that they are to be of the number of those who make full proof of the present fruits and privileges of salvation, and they shall not be disappointed.

Are there any such here to-night? any who run the race determinately and fleetly; who pass by, and get out of, and far beyond, the ranks of loiterers and them who are at ease? Are any of you running as if one alone were to obtain the prize? as if the gate of life were too narrow to admit any but yourself? Some of us will be taught the necessity for this, by seeing many draw back unto perdition. We might be taught it by Immanuel's words, 'Hold fast that thou hast, that no man take thy crown.' Ah! we'll get our crown taken unless we trample upon ease and sloth, and difficulty, in his name. BLESSED IS THE MAN THAT FEARETH ALWAYS, and who is thus, in continual trembling, led to draw from the fulness of One able to keep him from falling.

Now, may that jealous God, who brings down every high thing, and casts down every proud imagination, by 'the power whereby he is able to subdue all things unto himself,' *bring us down*, and cast us all into the dust before him; lest, being lifted up by pride, we touch, with Uzza's hand, the ark of the covenant; for then Uzza's judgments will surely break out upon us. Oh! that Jehovah would raise up, for his service in the ministry, men who will go about, taking their lives in their hands, counting not their life dear unto them. Precious, Lord, in thy sight, is the death of thy saints; and if it be so, why need they fear? they cannot lose life till the time appointed. Oh! for ministers in our beloved land, such as have never yet been seen, men who will go bound hither and thither, and will go all the more confidently in the Master's name, even when the Spirit testifies that 'bonds abide them.' Oh! for humbling in the Lord's sight, because of personal sin, to be creeping into the dust on account of it, and in view of thy glory, Lord Jesus. We see not thy matchless perfections, 'thou fairer than the sons of men,' and yet thou art ours, 'the chiefest among ten thousand, and altogether lovely!'

11

TRIAL MADE SWEET

[Perth, February 1844.]

'Patient in Tribulation.'—*Romans 12. 12.*

If, while earthly good is removed, divine consolation is given instead, the believer gets back an hundred-fold what he gave up, by receiving that which is an hundred-fold better.

What an example of this we have in Moses. He deliberately chose present reproach with the people of God, and then he straightway esteemed it 'greater riches.' Reproach is not a sweet thing in itself; it is only when it is Christ's reproach that it becomes sweet; and when it is thus suffered, believe the testimony of all the saints, that any suffering, when borne along with Christ, is sweeter than any joy enjoyed without him. Another thing that sweetens reproach, is when it is borne in company with the Lord's dear children: and indeed, there is just one company that it is good to be in, and that is the despised company of the Lord's children. Not that their outward circumstances, either always or often, make it pleasant to be with them. One does not naturally like to be shut up in the city where famine is raging, or in the dwelling infested by the plague: that cannot be desirable for itself, unless there is some circumstance apart from these that makes it so. Now, God's people are often in the greatest straits, sorely reduced, and seemingly forsaken; but it is best, it is safest, to be among God's people. And believe it, brethren, if there is any day when it is specially good to be among them, it is not when they are saying with Job, 'I shall die in my nest, and multiply my days;' and when all earthly things go so well with them that they have nothing more to wish for. It is safest, it is best, it is sweetest to be among them in dark and troublous times, when they find a hedge about their path, and when thorns are on the road; when they are wandering hither and thither in the valley of Achor, and are looking out at the door of hope. Theirs is now a waiting-time and a watching-time; a short day, or, as they are tempted to think it, a long day, of labour and of prayer, during which they have oft-times no comfort but that of the hope of brighter days to come. How often that expression forces itself on us, 'Thou shalt abide for me many days!' What a striking word! What a type of the faithful, constant self-dedication of the church, or of the believer, to his absent Lord! Ah! this reminds us, and reassures us that the marriage-covenant is not broken, it is not annulled. It was formed when the sinner gave his heart in solemn covenant to the Lord, and when the Lord himself said, 'Thou art mine;' shall it ever be forgotten, come what may? True, it is not yet complete, 'The top-stone' hath not yet been 'brought forth with shouting.' Believers have a time of trial given them meanwhile, an opportunity to prove their love for Immanuel; they are to be employed in waiting for him, and living to him; and he does not even now leave them comfortless. No, he comforts them in ways as various as their individual needs and desires.

Let us mention three of them. The first is *tidings of*

Himself, through the Word of God, which tells them all he was on earth, and much of what he is in heaven since he sat down upon his throne. The second way is by the visits of his Spirit, which are frequent, heart-supporting, and refreshing to the weary soul. And the third is the blessed hope of seeing him again; it may be soon, very soon; and it shall be a vision of him 'as he is,' whenever it shall come. By these and other means, after which we would earnestly entreat you to seek to profit—and he has infinite resources of grace and glory—he does support his church and carry her through the deepest waters, and across the raging surge, even beyond the river of death till he place her at his own right hand. And remember, my beloved friends, that it is no new thing for him to do this: nay, he can lead her through flames of fire, and seven-times heated furnaces, to the city of habitation, just as securely and as happily as by an ordinary path.

Oh! bear this in mind, that it is not an untried gospel that we are called to lean upon. It is no new thing to pass through fire and water before coming into the wealthy place prepared before the foundation of the world; nor is it an unbeaten path that the ransomed of the Lord have to pass over. It is a blessed thing when by trials the Lord leads his people on to his own future promised glory, and it is a safe thing when he leads them into the wilderness, because he has the power to carry them also through the wilderness, and out of the wilderness, all the journey through. Safe are they who are leaning on such an arm. They will be borne through, and, though they may have to seal their testimony with their blood, they will yet be borne testimony to. You may say, 'Why speak so much of these things?' Brethren, because we may need these things before we meet again—we cannot tell— yes, ere then the time may be come, when we shall have to enter into our chambers and shut the doors about us until calamity be overpast, and when, had we not such real supports as these to look to, we might be desolate enough. Ah! we would need to be having our anchor cast within the veil, to be learning to lay faster hold upon Jehovah's Word, and leaning on his faithful promises. What an amazing ground of consolation does that Word afford to the weakest saint! The Lord has provided the very surest and best foundation that his wisdom could have devised to invite and to secure the poor sinner's confidence. Build then upon it. Remember that 'he that endureth to the end, the same shall be saved.' 'Strait is the gate, and narrow is the way, and few there be that go in thereat. Many shall seek to enter in, and shall not be able.' 'He that loseth his life for my name's sake shall keep it;' keep it, defend, protect it unto life eternal. 'If any man serve me, him will my Father honour.'

12

THE BREAKER UP

[*Free West Church, Sabbath Evening, February 19, 1844.*]

'I WILL SURELY ASSEMBLE, O JACOB, ALL OF THEE; I WILL SURELY GATHER THE REMNANT OF ISRAEL; I WILL PUT THEM TOGETHER AS THE SHEEP OF BOZRAH, AS THE FLOCK IN THE MIDST OF THEIR FOLD: THEY SHALL MAKE GREAT NOISE BY REASON OF THE MULTITUDE OF MEN. THE BREAKER IS COME UP BEFORE THEM: THEY HAVE BROKEN UP, AND HAVE PASSED THROUGH THE GATE, AND ARE GONE OUT BY IT; AND THEIR KING SHALL PASS BEFORE THEM, AND THE LORD ON THE HEAD OF THEM.'—*Micah 2. 12, 13.*

This passage refers to ancient Israel, but its application does not end there. It applies to the salvation of every one who is delivered from the death and bondage of sin, by him here called 'The Breaker,' who is evidently no other than the Son of the mighty God. Three things we notice here—first, What is said of Israel, 'They have broken up, and have passed through the gate, and are gone out by it.' That has an application to all who are delivered; and to prepare the way for this, two other things must be noticed, and these refer, not to the people who go out, but to Jesus, their King,—'They have broken up, they have passed through the gate, and are gone out by it.'

You will ask, from what are they delivered? The language employed here refers to a state of captivity and

136

bondage, to persons shut up in a prison, encompassed by walls, gates, and bars. From this prison-house they come out. On the state of outward bondage to which the passage may refer, if taken literally, we have not time to dwell at present; but as applied to the state of an individual sinner, it evidently represents the man here to be in a state of imprisonment. When a citizen of any land commits a public offence against its laws, he is taken up, and, by the power of the law, kept in prison. So it is with the breakers of the law of God. What but the power of law is shewn by all our prisons and penitentiaries? What are these but so many assertions, made by the law of the country, that it has power over the acts of men, and so many provisions made by the statutes of the realm, for the safety of persons and of property—for the preservation of social order, and the maintenance of civil peace? So is it with the offender against God's moral government. Every claim made upon the creature rests on the divine law given in the Ten Commandments; and if we dared to place one part of Jehovah's testimony above another, we should call it the most important part of the Word of God—the only part of that Word which was written by his own finger; distinguished by him in this way.

Unless you have a right and distinct view of this, you can neither understand your awful state, nor God's glorious deliverance from it. Not till then will you see, that, as a human law pursues, imprisons, and keeps the offender bound, so the divine law accuses, pursues, apprehends, judges, condemns, and imprisons. Then it is that bonds are on the soul, and chains upon the conscience. They do not, indeed, bind the body, but they are stronger than any other, for the iron enters into the soul. The sinner is kept as in a prison held fast so that he cannot escape. If the bars were of brass, or iron, they might be broken; if they were adamant, they might be burst asunder; but the chain that binds him is a righteous sentence, passed by the Holy One. Who can alter the nature of justice? Its bond is stronger than omnipotence, since omnipotence will not, and cannot break it. Power cannot throw it down, for power is but the hand of justice, and inferior to it. Not so, indeed, on earth: what is right, and what is, are not always the same thing now. Power triumphs many a time over right; but even on earth, in a moral point of view, that which is right is infinitely superior to that which has merely power on its side. If omnipotence could prevail over justice at any time, to set her lawful captives free, it would put the triumph into Satan's hands! Is it not the very glory of the Lord, that his justice guides his power! The law has, in its own hand, a right to condemn and to destroy. Justice reigns and shines in God's government, through all his holy nature, and in his blessed will. Herein lies the strength of our prison. Take an illustration. When I sin, I am guilty. I am worthy of the wrath of the living God. Justice brings her accusations and lays them at my door, while, in her hand, is the warrant to destroy. And power stands back: it cannot, by whomsoever wielded, release me. Why? Because it was not against power that I sinned: it was justice that I wounded, it was holiness I grieved, and they must be satisfied, come what may of me. The illustration only gains strength as you widen the range from one guilty soul to a myriad. Come what may to all creatures in the universe, justice must be vindicated and glorified eternally.

By the Word of God, and from the experience of men, we know that in all ages, since the fall to this present day, there has come forth, from this dark and lawful prison-house, a holy band of delivered men, the ransomed church of God. They have broken up, passed through the gate, and have gone out by it. Yes; and we know, that at this hour there are in the midst of a world which lieth in the Wicked One, a company who have been breaking up, and passing through, coming out, by the open gates of righteousness, into present and eternal liberty from condemnation, vengeance, and eternal doom! They have broken up, and have passed through the gate. Observe, it is something done by them, not only done for them (as salvation, doubtless, is done wholly for us, in one sense); it is also done by an act of their own will,—an act, ungodly man, which you too must yet do, if ever you are to be saved,—an act, believing sinner, which you have already done. You are come out into a large place. How, then, did you this? How did you escape? We cannot understand it; and yet, you came out by your own act, you came out with the triumph and the confidence of a believing sinner, and you have walked in the light of God's reconciled countenance up to this hour. But how? Were not these walls of adamant, were not these barriers impassable, was not your soul undone? See, beloved, the Breaker! The heavenly Breaker is gone up before.

Three names are given to him in this single verse. There is, first, the incommunicable name, Jehovah—I am. This leader of the people is none other than 'the Man who is Jehovah's Fellow.' That is one name, but he has another, 'their King at the head of them,' even the King of kings. 'He hath on his vesture and on his thigh a name written, King of kings, and Lord of lords.' 'I will make him my First-Born, higher than the kings of the earth.' The third name given is the Breaker. See, now, it is Jehovah himself who has entered in and gone before; and he is called 'The

Breaker' for various reasons. First, that he has to break through many barriers. He opened the gate by which the ransomed of the Lord come forth from prison, and by which the church has a ready and constant access to the holiest of all. And how did he come forth?

We have told you of that prison-house, and of its security. We have told you that its walls are the righteousness of the law, holding the sinner under the curse of God. But how are these things ever to be taken out of the way? How shall holiness become the sinner's friend? How is divine justice to take the sinner's part, seeing that power can avail him nothing, supposing, which God forbid, it were brought over to his side. All is done by the Lord Jehovah. In a very few words we shall try to tell you how. He comes down from the heavens, and advances to the gates of justice; he undertakes to break them, by coming first into the prison itself, within its very walls. Among its poor inmates is heard the joyful sound, 'To us a child is born, to us a son is given.' To us the holy child Jesus appears, born among sinners, born in the prison, born within the gates of the condemning law, born of a human mother, born of a sinful creature. Not one whit better than other sinners was Mary. Of her was he born into a world condemned and perishing, and subject to the awful curse of God.

He did not enter the prison after he was brought up. No, he was *born* there; and not content with that, our King spends his life in the prison, dwelling here for more than thirty years. What was he doing all that time? Many seem to speak as if he had done next to nothing in these thirty years, and that his glorious work of redemption was not begun then; but that it was a very inferior part of his life on earth that we hear of when it is said that he lived unknown but as the carpenter's son—the child of Mary. But, ah! he was obeying the law, in satisfying all its demands and keeping it entire. Every bar, then, that made the prison secure, was impassable and indestructible, because each one was a bar of pure justice, and unspotted holiness, and eternal truth; and each one had a voice to cry, 'The soul that sinneth it shall die'; while the gates were bolted, so to speak, by the majesty and holiness of God.

Anything else would have been a setting aside of the justice of God, for the sake of a guilty worm,—which cannot be; therefore the Lord undertook to be the Breaker. Ah! Satan thought that the gates could not be broken, or at least, if they could, that it would serve his purpose even better; for it would be the triumph of power over right. But the Deliverer was a great King, and he was Jehovah all the time he was working out this deliverance for us. That was what made his work of infinite value; that was what enabled him confidently to undertake to pay all the price that justice could demand. He undertook to open wide the gates of brass, to buy them open, and to leave them open to the end of time, as gates of righteousness and gates of life! Oh, what an undertaking! For this he kept the holy law for three-and-thirty years; for this he laboured among the unbelieving Jews; for this he bore the united hatred of man and devils, aye, and even desertion from the Father himself. The work of his lifetime was to lay down the price of man's salvation, and to set open the gates of righteousness. Little did the world think what Christ was doing. Satan thought that he himself was triumphing in his own work of darkness; and in proportion as the Lord's work progressed, Satan thought it was going backward. When Satan thought the victory was won, Immanuel was actually putting the price into the Father's hand. So he lay in the grave till death could keep its royal Master no longer; for death had now no cord wherewith to bind him. On the resurrection morning, the Breaker arose a conqueror.

This was the Breaker coming up; and the reason why the bands of death were allowed to hold him was, that the strong bond of justice was around him. It was not man's power that crucified the Lord of Glory, it was an unseen power, the power of a sentence passed in a higher court. It was not the Jews, nor was it Pilate, that laid the chains upon him; it was the process pending at the bar of justice on high, in the name of sinners, *that* alone gave him into the power of death and the grave. But now, that sentence being executed, the grave could no longer hold him. He died once; but, behold! he is alive again.

I fear that few of us realise our need of this Saviour. Here the door is open, and now the message is to tell the wide world that all may enter; and to call upon all men to awake, arise, and flee from wrath to come. The prison is the very place where you have been born and brought up. You have lived in it too long to wish to escape from it. Yet listen to these precious words, 'The Breaker is gone up.' Yes; and he comes to you and asks you to go forth. The Lord comes up to the poor sinner, to every one whom he delivers; he comes by his word, by his divine power, by his servants, and by his Spirit. He awakens them; he arouses them, as he aroused the jailor at Philippi. Peter trembled when the angel came to him in the prison; but the Lord led him forth, and he found, to his amazement, that, instead of meeting with obstacles, every door was standing wide open for his escape. We need the Lord to come forth with us, to lead us by the hand. The door has stood open now for eighteen hundred years; but oh, how few come forth. How we need the Breaker still; we need him in the midst of us; we need his hand to touch the sleeping sinner, and take him by the hand. And all we have to do is to come among you to tell that the new and living way is open, and that if you will but come boldly up to it, come when it even seems bolted to your unbelieving eye, it will spring open of itself. Oh, that men were walking forth in multitudes into the freedom of the Lord! Where, oh where, is the freedom of the Free Church, if she is in bondage with her children, if they are not being made free by the Son of God?

13

WORDS OF WARNING

[Free St Leonard's Church, Perth, Sabbath Afternoon, February 19, 1844.]

2 Thessalonians, Chapter 2.

This chapter contains a most remarkable prophecy of the rise, progress, and final destruction of Antichrist; and we now desire to direct your attention to what prepared the world and the professing church in the first ages for being deluded by Antichrist, and to that which should also prepare the world in the end of time for receiving its delusions afresh. The apostle begins by warning the Thessalonian church of the danger they were in, of misunderstanding the directions which he had previously given them. They had been told that the Lord was at hand; and this was true, as the apostle meant it; but they had misunderstand him: they had been taking the times and the seasons out of the Father's hand, and had begun to set times for the accomplishment of prophecy. This was their error; and this epistle was written to entreat them not to be shaken or moved, as though the day of Christ were at hand. This warning equally applies to us in these days; for we are too apt to bring the fulfilment of prophecy down to the times in which we live. True, we are nearer to the end of time than the Thessalonians were; the coming of Christ is eighteen hundred years nearer than it was then. But still we have great need of warning regarding it. This is a time of trial in the church of God; a time when we cannot expect much outward peace or comfort; and therefore there is a great danger of men's groping about for consolation, laying hold of anything in that shape that comes within their reach, and oftentimes holding fast what is unreal: and then, again, it often happens, that when those things which they had taken up as certain do not come to pass, they are more and more discouraged.

The apostle begins by telling the Thessalonians about the Roman heresy, which should corrupt the professing church, until she should apostatise, and finally be made drunk with the blood of the saints. The character given here of this mystery of iniquity is very awful, and evidently applies to the Roman Antichrist. There are, doubtless, many Antichrists to which this description may have reference; but that it emphatically applies to Rome in the first instance, there can be no doubt. Notice what is set before us in the 10th, 11th, and 12th verses: 'And with all deceivableness of unrighteousness in them that perish; because they received not the love of the truth, that they might be saved. And for this cause God shall send them strong delusion, that they should believe a lie; that they all might be damned who believed not the truth, but had pleasure in unrighteousness.' This teaches us that God in righteous judgment would allow, and did allow Satan to put forth his power to deceive and ruin souls. Nothing is more remarkable than the *place* in which the abomination that maketh desolate was to be set up: it was not among the idolatrous heathen, nor among the open enemies of Christ, but in the *temple of God*, in the midst of the professing church itself; which teaches us clearly, that the judgments of the professing church are more awful than any other, because the sin of hearing the gospel without obeying it, is greater than any other. The deceitfulness of Rome is tenfold greater than any of the abominations of the heathen, and her judgments will be more tremendous. Why? To shew that there is no place where God so hates sin as in his own church. 'You only have I known of all the nations of the earth, therefore will I punish you for your iniquities.'

We may be preparing ourselves for that, remembering that, when judgment does begin at the house of God, it will be the most awful of all. There is no place where men will be more readily given over to delusion, and to the belief of a lie. There were few churches more honoured in early days than the church of Rome; and so now, because it has fallen from Christ, it has become a golden cup in the hand of Satan, by which he makes the nations drunk: that cup is going the round of the nations *now*, to the great amazement of many of the world's wise children. Many professors wonder at it too, and cannot comprehend how men, in the nineteenth century, should be drinking of all the delusions of the dark ages. They think they can easily, by their own natural powers and intellect, avoid all those deceits, and that it is a simple thing for men to judge, by natural wisdom, between truth and error. My dear friends, those who think so will be taught something else ere very long: nothing will save a man from being carried away by the deceivableness of unrighteousness, but the simple receiving of the love of the truth; and let it be remembered that none but those who have received the truth in the love of its most humbling, most Christ-glorifying, sinner-abasing, God-exalting parts, are in the least secure from being carried away by the mystery of iniquity, which seems threatening to overflow the whole land, and to take possession of the temple of God.

It is by the truth alone that men are saved; and a heart new created in them, to love, embrace, and keep close to the truth, is the only defence against error of every kind. It is not a wise head, but a sanctified heart, that will save a man from the most awful delusions, and from the most deep and wily deceits that Satan ever devised. See that you love the truth for its own sake, for the danger of being carried aside by error is never greater, than in a place where the work of God has been extensively carried on. When the Spirit ceases to work there, those people who have not the genuine love of the truth, lose their appetite for the plain preaching of it altogether. They are driven back and forward, as the chaff before the wind, and then, when the hour and power of darkness is, and when temptation rushes in, they are quickly carried away by Satan's devices, and by the lying wonders which he has received power to perform on the earth. The devil's power has been, is now, and will yet be so great, and the manifestations of it are so new and numerous, that the time appears to be drawing nigh when they will deceive, if it were possible, the very elect.

Men often think they will be saved from error by belonging to a particular congregation, association, or church, pure as they call it. They cry out, as Satan cries within them, 'The Church, the Church!' Not, perhaps, the Church of Rome, or even the Church of England, but still it comes much to the same thing—it is always *the church*, just as of old, 'The temple of the Lord, the temple of the Lord, the temple of the Lord are these!' Ah, brethren, beware, beware! No class is, perhaps, for this cause, so near to the strong delusion of Satan as those among whom great things have been done, and who have passed through glorious times of the Lord's right hand without receiving the truth. Look at the Jews, whom God singled out to be the object of his chief blessing. A remnant was indeed, saved according to the election of grace; but, as a nation, it was not so. Because they hardened their hearts, God sent them strong delusions, and Paul declares that their ears were dull of hearing, and their eyes they had closed, so that they could not see him to be very God, who was the only begotten of the Father. That delusion is not broken after eighteen hundred years, except in a very few cases comparatively. And shall the righteous Judge of all the earth act upon a different principle towards us now? He will not, he does not, as we have too fearful proof around us. Brethren, I warn you. We see not yet the end of these things: 'God shall send them strong delusion that they should believe a lie.' It is awful to be deluded in matters of eternal consequence, in things of the soul, where heaven and hell, life and death, are in the question; but how far more awful when God himself sends the delusion, for then, alas! it comes with the power of a divine commision; it comes over the soul without the opposition of a check or restraining power of any kind. It is the work of Satan as all the works of darkness are; it cannot proceed from the Father of lights, for in him is no darkness at all. Its cause and origin is far removed from him who is the fountain of life, and yet it is an act unopposed by him as the God of providence.

It was long a common delusion, that either no man could be really sincere in a bad cause, or in a false doctrine, or that, if he could be proved to be sincere, this was enough. Do you think that this passage would lead us to say that none can conscientiously hold a false doctrine?

No; for it is said 'that they should *believe* a lie;' shewing that men may be deceived in their belief, while it proves that their belief of a lie cannot save them from being condemned by it. While the termination of their sin is clearly pointed out, the fruitful cause of it is not hidden. It is declared to be twofold—the believing not the truth, and the having pleasure in unrighteousness. These sins involve many fearful consequences unimagined when they are committed. You may be safe, as you think, in a godly congregation, and yet commit these sins; you may belong to a pure church and yet commit them; you may have the gospel sound ringing in your ears and love to hear it and yet commit them. You have never yet believed Immanuel's testimony and when he himself drew near and appeared in his glory in this place and when his voice of majesty was heard and his glorious power seen in the sanctuary you never bowed to him, you never put the crown upon his head; multitudes of professing Christians rejected himself, and denied his work, or thought you did a great deal when you did not oppose it. And now you are twice dead, plucked up by the roots; no sermon touches you, no minister awakens your conscience, no warning ever gets near you. Awake! or Satan will rob you of your day of grace altogether, and ruin your precious souls.

'But we are bound to give thanks always to God for you, brethren beloved of the Lord because God hath from the beginning chosen you to salvation through sanctification of the Spirit and belief of the truth,' (verse 13). Chosen to salvation! Oh, that blessed word! The apostle thanked God; he did not thank himself, he did not thank them that they were faithful to their high calling; but he thanked God who had chosen them from the beginning, and called them to himself. This eternal purpose of God is your only security. And how precious what follows! They were not only chosen to faith and repentance, but chosen to complete salvation. The means used—the belief of the truth! The agent—Jehovah the Spirit! Yes, the living God takes a lump of the fallen Adam, quickens it, creates it anew, works faith in it, and brings it on to the end in view, the obtaining of the glory of our Lord Jesus Christ. And yet for this glorious salvation the unregenerate have no taste, though eternal life or eternal death is at stake. They look to things seen; their eye rests on present obstacles, and they *let salvation go!* they let it slip, and they are undone! Let the children of God also beware.

The devil is too cunning for you to withstand single-handed and alone. Hold fast by Christ, or he will lead you to the pit yet: he will take our life—he will lead us captive, and take our crown! He would take our Saviour from us if he could, and thus take our all.

Many of us seem to be, as it were, leaving Satan's artifices out of account; we seem to be thinking that somehow or other we shall slip into heaven, we know not well how. That was not Paul's expectation, and he knew well that it is far otherwise with God's people; and be' very sure that you will also have to encounter many an obstacle and many a difficulty more than you calculate on. 'If we suffer, we shall also reign with him.' 'To him that overcometh will I grant to sit with me in my throne, even as I also overcame, and am set down with my Father in his throne.' Are there any here who have got the spirit to overcome? any who are following the Lord fully? Or, are we not constrained to say, What a contrast to past days!—some becoming cold in their service, some leaving their first love, some falling into sin, some apostatising altogether, many losing their love of the truth, and going after new doctrines.

This brings us to notice, in verses 15th and 16th, first, an exhortation given, and then a prayer. 'Therefore, brethren, stand fast, and hold the traditions which ye have been taught, whether by word, or our epistle.' What tradition does he mean? you will ask. There are two kinds of traditions. One kind of man's making, all of which are to be abhorred and cast away; and another kind of traditions, which are God's traditions, and are to be held fast through life, and unto death, be the consequences what they may. The word 'tradition' has no mysterious or difficult signification; it means something delivered from one to another, —something handed down, whether from God to man, or from man to man. To the first of these we may ever safely cling: on the second many are now beginning to lean, and they will lean on them till they fall through them into destruction. Hold fast then the traditions which ye have been taught; not the traditions of men, not the traditions of Rome, not the traditions of your fathers, Christ's faithful martyrs though they were. No; leave that to Rome, leave that to English Puseyism. Your faith lies *here*, within the boards of this Bible. Your life is in that book, and especially in such parts of it as search deepest into your heart, and pierce furthest through your corruptions. The closer you keep to it, the further will you be from error.

'For there must also be heresies among you, that they which are approved may be made manifest among you.' You will see these spreading in different parts of the land. They will come, perhaps, into your own congregation, even amongst yourselves. I fear there may be something akin to this among you already. Hold God's truth, believer; take not up what is new either readily or strongly. Its novelty may for a time give it a charm; but novelty, novelty! is the cry of an Athenian fickle people, not that of the humbled, tried believer. He does not need this; he finds constant newness in the oldest truths; he finds a fresh and ever-flowing Spring of life in the Lord himself. He looks to Christ, and seeks to know and obey his will, and he has not time for more.

Beware of all doctrines which make you high-minded and puffed up, great talkers and expert reasoners, but which yet leave the soul as a dry and withered thing. Plain doctrines once satisfied you. I remember the time when they were your choicest portions in all the Word of God, but now I fear that *salvation*, *heaven*, *hell*, *judgment*, *eternity*, are not such weighty words as they used to be in your ears. Plain things have worn out of fashion; you have got beyond them; they are too simple and tasteless for you now. In those days the only thing that satisfied you was to hear old simple truths, and plain sermons about regeneration, or man's lost and ruined condition, or, perhaps, even more about Immanuel's righteousness, or the new heart, and the work of grace, whereby all old things pass away.

Listen to Paul's prayer for the Thessalonian church: 'Now our Lord Jesus Christ himself, and God, even our Father, which hath loved us, and hath given us everlasting consolation and good hope through grace, comfort your hearts and stablish you in every good word and work.' If that prayer were offered by your minister for you, and by you for yourselves, and answered, what a rich congregation would this be! I know that some of you don't wish to receive all that this prayer contains; some would like to settle down upon their lees, some would shrink from the testimony they are called on to make for Christ, and some would like to avoid the labour and fatigue of hard, every-day work; and some would spend their strength in controversy, because that warfare is so much more palatable and easy to the flesh than the good fight of faith. Brethren! be not hoodwinked out of your salvation, by thinking that you have found out a softer and an easier path to heaven than the old path, and the King's highway. There is no softer path to heaven, than that which still bears the foot-prints of the Man of sorrows. There has been no wider gate invented since the days when the Lord preached concerning it, in the land of Judea. It is the strait gate still, it is the narrow way still; and it must be trod barefoot, to be trod at all. We must agonise in order to enter it at all; it takes many a conflict before the gate yields to our hand, for it is strait, or rather, it takes many a conflict with the sin that we would fain be allowed to carry with us. Do you say you find the way hard? Oh! don't stop short of eternal glory, for the sake of a hard road to it. The Lord himself will put you on it. The Lord will give you everlasting comforts in it. Think not of making a bed of ease, on the road which Immanuel strewed with groans, and sighs, and prayers, and tears! Think it enough if you have the Three-One God to meet with by the way, and besides that seek nothing, but be thankful now and then to be meeting with some weary pilgrim like yourself, who can tell, from a deeply-taught and deeply-humbled soul, of the goodness and lovingkindness of your covenant God.

Trust not much for your soul's profit to the constant talking about matters connected with religion, which we now hear so much of. You cannot go into a steamboat or a coach now-a-days without hearing something of that kind, and yet, my dear friends, we do not find that true religious conversation is more common: on the contrary, it is much more uncommon than it was. It is always the church, the church! that we hear of. There is more Puseyism in that cry than we think; and, meanwhile, our need of grace in the heart is forgotten. There is little about us of that which puts men in mind that there is still a heaven, and a hell, and a glorious, living, reigning Christ. There seems at present to be a blight lying on ministers and people; little good is done; eternity is not brought near to our own souls, and how can we bring it near to the souls of others?

Wait then on the Lord, in this time of deadness and desertion; for, though multitudes are perishing, and though the world is fast asleep, yet there are still some, if not many, precious souls quietly and silently creeping into the kingdom of God, by the strait gate. And though noisy professors may be abusing the present outward circumstances of the church, to their own hindrance, and though the crowd of worldly men may sink yet deeper in their forgetfulness of God, use you this season lawfully, and do not make a curse of what God intends for a blessing; hide for a little moment safe under his wings from the fear of evil. Seek righteousness, seek meekness; it may be ye shall be hid in the day of the Lord's anger.

14

THE VALLEY OF VISION

[*Preached in St Leonard's Church, Perth, on Wednesday evening, March 11, 1840, to a densely crowded audience.*]

Ezekiel 37.

There is so much in this chapter, that we cannot attempt to explain equally all parts of it; but shall merely make a few observations on what appear to be the principal objects offered to our consideration, remaining longer or shorter on each as the Lord may direct.

The first thing which seems pointed out, is the valley of vision itself, as it is called in another place, and of which the context clearly shews us the meaning. The valley filled with bones, represents a place filled with the remains of soldiers once alive. It was as the charnel-house of Israel, full of the slain, who, after death, had undergone the process of dismemberment and dissolution. Their bodies had first become lifeless, then suffered corruption, putrefaction, and decay; and not only so, but the very flesh had entirely left their bones, and they had become bleached, and whitened, and separated one from another; the ligaments, sinews, and joints being all broken, and everything but the actual bones dissolved and disappeared. The bones were 'very many and very dry.' What more complete picture of desolation and death could be given; and yet it is not a picture in the least too vivid of the state of moral death into which man has since the fall been sunk. He is dead, as it is explained in Ephesians,—'and you hath he quickened who were dead in trespasses and sins.'

Now, this doctrine, though allowed, is seldom believed and seldom acted on. We come to your city and tell you that you are dead, that it is a valley of dry bones; we call on you to flee and escape from 'the city of destruction,' and you are angry, you will not believe it, but you cry out, 'It is defamation.' Is it defamation? Then cast it upon the Lord Jehovah. But if you do, take warning of this, for you must abide by the consequences of resisting his word. He has shewn us, by the vision of the valley of dry bones, the state of unregenerate man, and we must see by that word that the comparison is just—'there is no health, no life in us,' 'we are full of wounds, and bruises, and putrefying sores.' We are first dead by our relation to Adam, our father according to the flesh, having in him sinned, and thus come under the fearful condemnation of the broken covenant of works, and so made liable to the wrath and curse of Almighty God. Original sin, or the sin of our nature, therefore, seems to conclude us all in death. The spirit of life is taken from us, and the progress of decay is day by day increased by every actual transgression. It takes away even from the form which remained after the life was extinct, until, at length, our whole spirits and souls become corrupted and fast approaching the last stage of decay, illustrated by the dry bones.

One of the effects of our being dead is that we have lost the image of God, so that, with regard to that, we have become wholly unprofitable, like dry bones, in his sight. Man was at first created that he might be a mirror to reflect the glories of Jehovah. Now is that image entirely defaced, and another image is put on his defaced and disfigured soul. He no longer is holy, just and true, but is (to use Scripture language) at enmity with God. What a thought is this enmity! How strange that the creature should ever have come to such a height of folly, of madness and iniquity, as to rise up and rebel against the God that made him, the God that shall judge him, the God that must for this condemn him to the torments of hell.

Now, such are you all, every one. This is what the true minister of Christ sees. He beholds you standing on the brink of a tremendous precipice, beneath which hell's gulf lies; he sees that unless God stretches out an omnipotent and a saving arm, you must drop into it. The servant of God, knowing and feeling this, cannot rest till he endeavours to make you aware of your danger. He cries out to you, beseeching you to consider; he must pull you away, drive you away from the edge of the pit, try to save you, that he may bring you home to God.

But let us now consider the chapter before us. First, the prophet says, 'The hand of the Lord was upon me.' This shews us what a real call to the ministry is. There are many calls spoken of among men, but this shews us there is but one. 'The hand of the Lord was upon me.' This primarily alludes to his exalted commission as an inspired prophet at the actual moment in which he wrote, but in an inferior, though not less real sense, does the Spirit descend on every preacher of Christ crucified, and call him to his work, whether in earliest infancy, in boyhood, or in riper manhood.

'And set me down in the midst of the valley, which was full of bones, and caused me to pass by them round about.'

This is what God always does when he intends to make any man an honoured instrument for the salvation of souls,—He takes him out into the world, takes him all round the valley, and shews him that it is 'full of bones, very many and very dry.' He leads him from city to city, and, it may be, from country to country. Very often, when ordinary Christians are thinking that people are unhealthy and require amendment, they are not well, but their case is not very bad; the true servant of Christ sees that they are dead, that their case is desperate, that they are not only diseased and wounded, decaying and putrifying, that they are dead men, and that their bones only remain to shew they are men at all. It is a dark, melancholy spectacle to such a person to look abroad on the world; he sees nothing but a valley of bones, dismembered and decaying, and he mourns over them, and whether he may disclose it to those around him or not, there is an inward fountain of tears ever flowing over. He weeps over souls of men.

The Lord then said to the prophet, 'Can these bones live?' This, again, is a question put by the Lord to every minister, to see what manner of spirit he is of. Now, some ministers answer, 'We think they can live. Many are diseased, but we shall preach much to them, we shall pray much with them; they have been born of Christian parents, brought up in a Christian country; they were brought to baptism in their infancy, they drank in the gospel truths with their mother's milk, were early brought to know the Word, learnt it on a mother's knee, learnt it by a father's side, they have been instructed in the doctrines of their holy Protestant faith, and, later in life, have been duly examined by a good minister, who has passed them as communicants worthy to sit down at the table of the Lord, and therefore we think that they can live.' But what does the faithful minister of the gospel say in reply to such a question? He puts it back to God, saying, 'Lord, thou knowest.' Ah! it is a blessed thing when believers learn to do this; whenever a hard question is asked them, or a hard doctrine held out for their belief (many are the questions thus proposed), they honour God by simply giving it back to him, and praying, 'Teach me.'

Again He said, 'Prophesy upon these bones, and say, O ye dry bones, hear the word of the Lord!' It is the duty of every minister to preach the Word of the Lord; and this command to preach the Word to *dry* bones even, alone encourages us to do so. I have often said, and still oftener thought, that I might just as well, and with as much hope of success, go and preach to the gravestones in your Greyfriars churchyard as come here to you—knowing that man can do nothing at all. 'Why, then,' some say, 'do you preach? Why do you go to church, why then do you tell men to come to Christ if they cannot repent, which you yourselves allow and say they never can?' Because it is commanded; and this very command is our authority, this command is our support, this command is our encouragement. When ministers get a sight of the valley of vision, and of the bottomless gulf into which bone after bone is sinking, they do feel that it is of importance that they should warn and alarm sinners; and then alone do they preach for death, preach for eternity, preach for the judgment-seat, preach for heaven, and preach, too, for hell. He at once goes, then, to call to the dry bones, and often, too often, does it without effect; but when he has done so, and spoken the words of the Lord, according to the will of God, then the Almighty himself speaks to them through him, saying, 'Behold, I will cause breath to enter into you, and ye shall live; and I will lay sinews upon you, and will bring up flesh upon you, and cover you with skin, and put breath in you, and ye shall live, and ye shall know that I am the Lord.'

'So I prophesied as I was commanded; and as I prophesied there was a noise, and behold a shaking, and the bones came together, bone to his bone.' The prophet obeyed the command of Jehovah, hopeless as his endeavours might have appeared to him, and, lo! a shaking among the dry bones. Sinners first begin to be concerned, then anxious about their state, and then alarmed, and *that* sometimes so greatly, that it cannot be concealed in their outward deportment. Sleep flies from them, and tears are their portion night and day. But is this not very natural? and yet, when it is so, it is often called enthusiasm and madness. In Dundee lately, something of this kind was witnessed, and it was therefore denounced as not being the true work of God, because some cried out and wept bitterly, groaning as they felt themselves under the dominion of Satan, and got a sight of sin in their own hearts. It was on that occasion said by a well-known and very godly minister, from the north of Scotland, who visited Dundee in order to assure himself whether it were, indeed, the Spirit of God who was working there, 'When bone comes to bone, will there be no shaking heard?'

And what time is more likely for such feeling as this, as when numbers of sinners are at once and together convinced of sin. Ah! will there be no extraordinary feelings, no excitement more than usual, when men first awake from the sleep of death, when they first see that hell from which they are escaping, and whose iron gates are newly barred behind them? No commotion when they first catch a glimpse of their heaven, to which they are joyfully turning that newly-opened eye? Will there be no heart-stirring emotions when they see sin, not as condemning them, but as wounding the Crucified? If there is no deep feeling, my dear friends, whether it be inward or outward, when a mind is renewed, and undergoing that thorough change which must accompany regeneration, there is great danger, we think, of the apparent change not having been real. A man *must* feel at such a time; it is impossible but that he should feel, and that with a depth unknown to him before.

After the coming of bone to bone, the next thing that happened was the covering of the bones with sinews, and with flesh, and with skin. The body formerly decayed, was renewed; but ah! 'twas lifeless still. I fear many present have got this length, and yet are not saved. Some of you have been getting sinews and flesh on the formerly naked bones. That is, you have been seeing your deformity in part, and you begin to perform neglected duties, to attend meetings, to study the Word of God with regularity, to go through your morning and evening devotions punctually; all around you, perhaps, are admiring the change, and you yourself are convinced that you are changed; you have come to ministers, and followed them: Ah! you are *our* converts, and not the Lord's. Beware of this—*beware of this!* If you are only the converts of ministers, woe, woe be to you, and woe be to us if we deceive!

I remember to have read of the great Whitefield, that one day, as he was returning from preaching, he overtook a man, who was intoxicated, driving a cart. When the carter recognised Whitefield, he called out, 'O Mr Whitefield, is that you? I'm glad to see you. I'm one of your converts.' 'Yes,' said Whitefield, 'I see you are one of *my* converts, and not one of the Lord's.' Ah! what good will it do you in the day of judgment, that you have been outwardly changed, if the Spirit have not changed your hearts? Now, we don't deny that the change which has taken place is good; but don't rest there—don't rest in that outward form. I doubt not, 'tis lovely to look on; ah, 'tis fair and beautiful. No eye, perhaps, sees a defect in the newly-formed character, in the virtues so carefully cultivated, in the duties so scrupulously performed. No human eye detects the faults. All are deceived, and admire the change.

Thus, when the spirit has just fled from its earthly tenement, the body sometimes appears alive still for a little, and the unpractised eye says, 'Ah, I see no difference. My brother is not dead. The expression of intelligence and wonted sweetness plays around the lips. Still I can see no change.' Yes, that form is fair, is ofttimes passing lovely; the colour that once glowed upon the cheek still tinges it, perhaps, in death; the chiselled features have not suffered the slightest change; the eye is not yet dimmed, the smile has not yet left the lips that never spoke but in love; and yet—yet—the eye that penetrates deep, the discerning eye, sees that death is there, sees a pallid hue fast o'erspreading the whole countenance, sees that, though the eye is there, no life is darting forth from it. And there is a death-like chill fast coming over the members of that frame; while the eye looks, it is all the while sealed in death, and you know that a body such as that, a body on which decay has, as yet, made no inroads, is as ready for the coffin as the dry bones are, is just as ready for the grave as the putrefying corpse by its side. Though no hideous deformities which disfigure the one, are to be traced in the other, both are dead. There is no difference as to any power of action or of thought. And so, if the Spirit of God has not begun, and is not carrying on the work of conversion, the most amiable, dutiful, and devoted individual, is not more *alive*, more endued with the Spirit of life, than the man who is sunk in guilt and in crime. Far be it from us to say, that there is no difference as to *this* world. The man who has openly sinned, alike fallen a victim to dissipation and to vice, is like the decayed body or the dry bones, or, perhaps, in that last stage of all, just crumbling into dust. But what we desire for you, above all, is, that ye be not deceived. We fear there are many (and it is natural that such should be the case) who are imagining themselves to be indeed converts to Jesus Christ, who will soon, very soon, fall away, and whose souls, much changed as they seem, are dead, entirely dead, dead to God, dead in sin. Many outward marks of a child of God are in the character, but ah! there is an icy coldness in the heart. It beats not with love to God, beats not with heavenly love to man, beats not at all. The veins, the sinews, the joints are there, all in lovely proportion; but there is no life, no blood, no heat.

Hatred to God lies hid within: you imagine it is gone; but ah! in the case of many, it is not driven out of the soul at seasons like this; it is not driven out, it is merely *driven in*. Outward circumstances are pressing you so hard, that even Satan may not dare to let that fearful enmity appear. And so, assaulted on all sides, it retires, and retires, and retires, till it is concentrated in the heart, taking up its dwelling in the very strongest fortress, in the citadel of the soul, and there it remains, and there it is chilling and congealing all, and so it will continue to do, till it consumes your fancied religion, and torments you so completely, that it will soon, very soon, seal you in the cold sleep of death. You are polishing and beautifying the exterior of your sepulchres but they will at last be discovered to be full of dead men's bones, of decay, and of corruption. The kernel, as it were, is still as hard as ever, as unbroken as ever, though it lies within a beautiful and finely-painted shell.

Now, what is to give you life, animation, power, to serve God acceptably—what can do this? 'Lord, *Thou* knowest.' The prophet sees that all his labour is vain, as far as having raised up living men is concerned. 'There is no breath in them.' 'Then said he unto me, Prophesy unto the wind, prophesy, son of man, and say to the wind, Thus saith the Lord God, Come from the four winds, O breath, and breathe upon these slain that they may live. So I prophesied, as he commanded me,'—*as he commanded me*. Ah, here is the strength of the minister of the gospel. He prays for the Spirit of the Lord, that it would come down and bless the Word, causing the seed to spring up and bear fruit; and when the Spirit does accompany the words, how marvellous are its effects. It breathes on the slain, they live, and 'stand on their feet, an exceeding great army.' It is sad when ministers do not come from the secret place to the pulpit, for then they do not come with the fulness of the Spirit. Pray much for us, that all who preach the gospel be much in prayer, yea, live in prayer for the descent of the Spirit, and the blessing of the Holy Ghost, or else we may as well not preach to you at all. Pray that we may all see the bones to be 'very many, and very dry,' and thus be filled with compassion on perishing multitudes, and declare to them the whole counsel of God as for eternity.

As scarcely any time remains, we ask you but one question, Have you any grounds for believing that you have received the Holy Ghost? or have you not so much as heard whether there be any Holy Ghost? If you have not, the consequence is that you are still unconverted, unsaved, for you cannot have believed on the Lord Jesus Christ, without the Spirit of Jehovah. The error of some is, that they trust to themselves in part, while they likewise in appearance trust in part to Christ—that is, they believe they are obtaining strength from Christ. They are growing on their own roots, and in their native soil. This will never do. You will never become true converts till you are quite translated from the soil of nature to the soil of grace. You must be taken out of self altogether, and be engrafted into the true vine, even Immanuel, and from him you will receive strength, support, and consolation. Do you want life from the dead? He is our life, he is light, he is love. Join yourselves to him in a perpetual covenant, which shall not be broken. If you have received Christ, he will be precious to you. If he is your portion, you will want, you will desire, no other.

When a poor man comes to a great inheritance, he will not seek to keep possession of the little hut or cottage which he formerly inhabited. That would be given up to the first beggar who comes to ask it. He will rather be glad to get rid of what reminds him of a state of wretchedness. And so with those who have obtained Christ, and seen his glory. You don't need the world, or anything in it, to complete your bliss; you don't want gay amusements, and trifling pleasures; you don't occupy yourselves with ornaments, and studied dress, and apparel. You say, 'We don't need the world's amusements; we have got Christ. Take your world, take its pleasures and its gains.' The believer does look with contempt on the world, and on its trifling occupations, saying, 'What have I to do any more with idols? Henceforth would I glory in nothing but the cross of my Lord Jesus Christ, by which the world is crucified unto me, and I unto the world.' You have got Christ, and with him his holiness, his righteousness, his consolations, his glory, his Father, his heaven. 'For all things are yours.' You have got Christ for the hour of need, Christ for life, Christ for death, Christ for prosperity, Christ for adversity, Christ for trials, Christ for bliss, Christ for judgment, Christ in time, and Christ through all eternity. And what need you more? 'Christ is yours, and ye are Christ's, and Christ is God's.'

Will any one of you go away without him to-night? If you do, you cannot go away without Satan, Satan in your bosom; and you are just cherishing the viper which will cut and sting you to all eternity. We ask you this question, in the view of that great meeting, that glorious assembly before the great white throne, from which there will not be a single absentee, though there are now so many absent from a throne of grace. You shall be there, I shall be there, all now absent shall be there, and we shall give account to God. The only question then will be, Who is Christ's? Who?

I speak to you in view of that nearer parting, which must soon take place between us, when we, who speak, can no longer speak to you, for we are come here only for a short period, to stand and preach the gospel, and tell that Christ is free, that salvation is free, that heaven is free, to all. When one city falls asleep, we must just go to another (and many other cities are eager for the glad news), and tell them too that it is free to them. These meetings which, praised be God, have been blessed to many, are now necessarily nearly at an end; and will you, who have come night after night, and week after week, and so patiently listened to us, part from us to-night without listening to Christ, without coming to him, as many have been all along doing? You have received us with the greatest kindness, and shewn us, in every possible way, that you would do much for us; but will you not come to Jesus, and come out of yourselves?

Here, in this heart, there is no good thing, nothing but emptiness, pollution, corruption, and sin; but yonder! ah, yonder! all fulness dwells. You may look within all your lives, and you will find nothing, nothing but guilt to be repented of, depravity to condemn; but yonder, in Jesus, all righteousness, all peace, all love abide: if you will come to him, they are yours. Now, won't you look, won't you live? Some of you have been long kept in doubt, and darkness, and despair; and why? Is it God's will that it should be thus? No, no! Then whose fault is it, if not your own? You've been trying to convert yourselves, trying to effect a change; and so long as you try that, you will never be saved, you will never have peace. Just try, now, to look out of yourselves, and *into* Christ, and up to Jehovah's throne of grace, and up to the blood on the mercy-seat; and while looking, try to get very low, infinitely low; for what other posture befits the worm Jacob, when he approaches his great Creator, his Eternal Judge? Yet fear not; for even the worm Jacob may look up with complete confidence, for he is commanded to look in Christ, and by Christ, and to Christ alone. Come in then, come in to Christ. The neighbouring villages are, many of them, crying out for Christ. Will you not be provoked to jealousy? will you not join them? Oh, that the whole city would lift up its gates, that the King of Glory might enter in.

15

THE TEN VIRGINS

[*Preached in Moulin Parish Church on Sabbath evening, September 6th, 1840. In the forenoon of the same day, Burns preached in a tent to the people who were seated in the Churchyard. Many of the higher classes were present who were not likely to have a second opportunity of hearing him, unless attracted by that discourse. He was almost unable to get through the service. He said afterwards, that the adversary of souls had been at his right hand the whole time; and that each statement he sought to make from the Word of God, seemed to be contradicted by a voice within as soon as made. At night he preached as follows to a congregation of country-people in the same place; the emptied vessel was filled to overflowing.*]

Matthew 25. 1–13.

'Then shall the kingdom of heaven be likened unto ten virgins, which took their lamps and went forth to meet the bridegroom.' 'Then': this expression shows us that the following parable is prophetical, relating to an event which shall take place at a future period, which, if you look at the close of the last chapter, you will find to be the coming of Immanuel to judge the world in righteousness. This event happens in one sense to every man at the hour of death, but it is his second coming, when he shall come to *all*, to judge all, to condemn all who believe not, that is here spoken of; it is an event to which the believer looks forward with joy unspeakable. Now, how many are there

here who can say they are hasting to his coming? I heard of a little child, who has been lately, we trust, indeed brought to Jesus, who seemed already to enter into this feeling. She said to her Sabbath school teacher, 'Oh! I'm wearying to see Christ.' Can you say this? Ah! can you say it, Christians? This expresses the feeling of the faithful followers of Christ, when they are not in a very dead state; they are all 'wearying to see Jesus,' 'whom, having not seen, they love.'

'Unto ten virgins.' This number seems to have been merely chosen from the circumstance of that being a usual number of persons to wait for the bridegroom on occasion of a marriage. It is said 'they took their lamps.' This expression is employed to represent the profession of religion made by Christians. By the lamps of profession we understand more than it is sometimes supposed to mean. What is a professing Christian? Who is considered now as a consistent professor? One would think that the nineteenth century had widened the gate to heaven. In the idea of too many among us, he is a consistent professor whom his neighbour cannot charge with open violation of the moral decency of the community in which he dwells. If a man is not a drunkard, if he does not steal, if he has not lifted the murdering knife, if he is a good neighbour, and, in short, a peaceable member of society, that man is a Christian, and it would be uncharitable to doubt it. At what point of degradation, of sleep of death, have we then arrived, when this is the standard of Christians in a Christian land? Yet there is many a name in the communion roll that never was inscribed in the Lamb's book of life; there is many a baptised face that never got the Spirit's seal upon its forehead; there is many a one looked up to and esteemed by men and considered as a true believer, who never was missed from his place on the Sabbath in church, that stands also on Satan's catalogue for the hottest place in hell. But all this does not nearly amount to the profession of the foolish virgins, for the difference between them and the wise virgins does not seem to have been discovered till the last scene of life. They all went forth to meet Jesus.

This going forth implies much more than is included in a profession. The foolish virgins, as well as the wise, come out from the world and take up their lot with the followers of Immanuel. Going forth to meet him, implies expecting him, waiting for him, looking forward to his coming, deriving joy from the thoughts of it, and the hope of his glory. There is very often nothing in such characters by which they can be distinguished from the true servants of Jesus, nothing in their outward conduct, nothing in the account they give of their experiences, by which it can be discovered. To the eye of man, the difference is often unapparent. The features of their character, their feelings, seem identical. It is a great mistake to think that among the foolish virgins, none know anything of experimental religion of a natural kind. There can be no doubt, that such persons as are here described, may know much of this.

But here there is a clear distinction made between the two classes: 'five were wise, and five were foolish.' There is a difference in the eye of God. The wise are his own elect, his redeemed, his chosen, his reconciled children; and the others—poor, deluded souls, little do they think whose they are, little do they think that Satan binds them, holds them fast, possesses them as his slaves, just as much as he does those careless, thoughtless sinners that are lying contented in his chains! They little know that, honoured and loved as they are, they are Satan-bound, Satan-deluded, Satan-enslaved, Satan-possessed. It is fearful to see men rushing headlong, sunk in crime, down to hell: but who can imagine the state of those who are living and dying in the hope of a heaven they are never to enter, and without a single fear of the hell to which they are now condemned?

What, then, distinguishes the one from the other? One certain distinction exists between the saint in the very lowest state into which a saint can sink, and the sinner in the highest state of outward perfection to which a hypocrite can rise. The difference is just this: in the one heart God reigns, and in the other Satan reigns. In the unregenerate heart of the professor, Satan may have assumed, as he constantly does assume, the character of an angel of light, but still it is Satan, in whatever form, that is on the throne. The influences of the Spirit of grace which operate on his heart, striving with him in a manner common to all sinners, are entirely subordinate and uninfluential. Christ is always knocking at the door, calling him by his providences, calling him by his love to man, and the poor sinner thinks he belongs to Christ, thinks he is getting grace from Christ, thinks he is saved, while Satan has still the citadel, the dominion, the command.

In the regenerate heart, it is not so. Immanuel reigns. He has assumed entire command, and however much the saint may sink into ungodliness, into temptation, into sin, Immanuel holds him in his hand, whence no devil shall ever tear him. Satan is not less active in this man's heart than in the other, but he is dethroned. The very moment that Immanuel first entered that heart, he took the command of it, he sat down for ever on the throne, he took the crown, he took the sceptre, and the devil was cast down for ever. *That* man's heart is no longer in the power of the devil; he comes often to the door, pays many a visit, and makes many a loud, boisterous knocking from without; but he does not dwell, he does not reign there, it is his dwelling-place no more. The Spirit of Jehovah fills his room, and spreads around the graces of Immanuel. He is often tempest-tossed, rudely and severely tempest-tossed, so rudely, that he thinks he is sinking altogether; but grace, however weak, is still there; there, ready to kindle up afresh, to burn into a flame.

We do not say that those characters represented by the foolish virgins never receive grace; we believe that there are some operations of the Spirit common to all; in other words, that there is such a thing as common grace. For instance, take the case of a man under convictions of sin, which never issue in saving conversion. That there are such cases, no one can deny; all have heard of it, most have met with it in their own experience. I daresay there are some among yourselves, brethren, who recollect such cases in the revival of Moulin, forty years ago. I have seen such cases myself. A man, during an awakening of great power, sees one and another, and another, of his former associates change, and become thoughtful and anxious, and, in short, turning to the Lord with full purpose of heart; he says, 'What is the meaning of all this? what has come over them?' By degrees the man sees that it is he who is mad in continuing unconcerned, and that they are in their right minds. The man is convinced. The sins of his former life come crowding round him in dread array. Past iniquities take hold on his affrighted conscience, with all the pungency and all the bitterness of newly committed sin; he feels wrath to be his portion, and he is bound down under the full weight of the approaching wrath of God.

It was only last Friday, as often before, that I witnessed such a scene. I saw men, young men, strong in body and mind, almost overwhelmed with a sense of their guilt, and of the justice of their eternal condemnation. But I saw cases too at Perth, where the feelings were thus aroused, and where persons have been so overcome by a discovery of their present actual state in God's sight, as children of wrath, that it has almost been too much for them to bear. Many a sleepless night have they passed, many an anxious day, many watchings, many tears, has it cost them, and this led them to do many things, to attend meetings regularly, to read the Bible, and to pray; and after a time they seemed really to find peace and joy in believing. But, ah! friends, what are some of these become? The dog has returned to his vomit again, and the sow that was washed to her wallowing in the mire. These very men have I seen returning, with more greediness than ever, to the gratification of their lusts. The outward man was changed, the character was formed anew, but the nature, the old man, the swinish nature, still remained. It had never been removed. It had never given place to the Spirit of Jesus. But can we think that this change was the work of the mere natural heart, of the sleeping, dead conscience? No, beloved brethren, no man who reads the Bible can suppose it.

Common grace is often given without the new nature, and that grace is often given to change and improve the outward character. But why was this grace asked from God? It was just to exalt the creature, to exalt self, to exalt the sinner, and to cast down the Saviour. It is not to glorify Jesus that such a man asks grace, but just that he may turn it against the Giver. He kneels below mercy's golden sceptre, just that he may, as it were, wrest it from Immanuel's hand; he has got grace, but then he has never got Christ. You have all heard of the common fable of the jay, that tried to imitate the peacock, by getting itself all covered with its beautiful plumage, Now, the persons to whom we have been alluding, just remind us of the poor bird in this fable. They have asked grace, only that they might deck out and adorn the hideous mass of corruption that lies concealed within; they use it to adorn themselves, and never simply to glorify Jesus.

Not so with renewed hearts! The Spirit of God has shewn them not only the future punishment of sin, but it has shewn to them the gigantic strength and power of prevailing inward corruption. It has shewn them that they must be entirely changed, entirely renewed, born again, or they must perish, they must die, they must be damned; they see, as it were, all help cut off from every side, above, beneath, all around. There is nothing, nothing but a fearful looking for of wrath and fiery indignation, which shall devour the adversaries, and must devour them. Their iniquities cover their heads, and they sink in the mire and in the deep waters; all the Lord's billows go over them, so that they cannot look up.

Such a soul feels as if he had been cast down over a precipice, whose base arises from perdition's gulf, and that he might just as soon catch the air, grasp it in his hand, and thus save himself, as conquer the heart disease that rages within, or behold a reconciled Father in the Avenger of sin. This is no exaggerated picture of human destitution; for oh! a guilty sinner is too heavy a material to fly up through the ether of holiness to the glorious presence of Jehovah, or reach the thrice holy precinct of the heaven of heavens. He feels this, and he can never soar aloft unless borne on the eagle pinions of Immanuel's unspotted righteousness.

There lies the grand distinction between the wise and the

foolish virgins. The wise are united to Christ. The others are not. *Union to Christ!* Here is the difference, here is the distinction, here is the life-giving principle, that has been inspired into the new created heart by the Holy Spirit. Here is the principle, without which, whatever be his profession, whatever be his hopes, whatever be his actions, the sinner is unprofitable, dead, unsaved, unsanctified, condemned. Union to Jesus is the humble Christian's life, his hope, his all; leave him but this, and you may take what you will away from him. It makes his trials, his afflictions, his losses, his sorrows, his griefs, not only supportable, not only endurable, but precious, sweet, a cause of thanksgiving, a matter for glory, just because in them—in the very severest, in the very hottest—that union is always the more closely cemented. The furnace burns, burns, burns, but ah! it touches not his union with Immanuel. The hotter the furnace burns, self, and sin, and pride, die out and waste away, and are sometimes so nearly consumed, that the soul forgets that there is any other in the wide universe but Jesus. Self is all but destroyed, for one desire and another is checked, cut off, and consumed; a rebellious will has been so crushed, so broken, so bended, so moulded to the image of him to whom alone it has clung in the storm, that for a time it seems to have forgotten to be rebellious. For the time no other will is known than his, who, while he wounds, is tempering every trial with a hand gentle and tender, and filling up every place that is left vacant of its creature tenant, with a Creator's infinite love.

The foolish professor, as one said, is like a tree, bending to one side, leaning over on the support of another, whereas the Christian, not only leans on Christ, but he is like a slip of a tree grafted into another tree, he has come off his own root, he has been cut off completely, and grafted deep into Christ. It is quite necessary that the sinner should be entirely reduced to self-despair; for nothing but self-despair can make him feel his need of a Saviour, and the Holy Spirit brings every savingly convinced sinner into this state. Helpless and lost, he lies down as it were, to die, and feels that no efforts of his own can ever in the least even enable him to arise and lay hold on the rock of salvation. He feels that, unless Jehovah, by an act of absolute, free, sovereign, and resistless grace, lay hold of him, raise him up and translate him from Satan's power to that of Christ, he must die. He sees that, unless reconcilement begin on the part of Jehovah, he can never be reconciled, and thus he is brought by the Spirit to lay aside all those things, which formerly he was vainly trying to perform and to work out in his own soul, and just simply to come out of himself into Jesus. Christ first apprehends the sinner; having elected him, he begins by the drawings of his grace to attract him to himself; and then, as the natural consequence, the first strength thus received is employed by the thankful penitent in loving, serving, and adoring his divine Redeemer. The newborn babe is cherished, cared for, and tenderly watched by its mother, while unconsciously it lies, folded in her arms, insensible of her love. But whenever it begins to grow a little, and to get even a little strength, its first natural action is to clasp its little arms round the neck of its mother. Just so is it with the poor sinner. Jesus, long before *he* is aware of it, says, 'I have called thee by thy name, thou art mine.' He continues by his providence and love to incline the sinner, till at last, coming willingly to him, and no longer desiring to rebel, he begins to love such a Saviour, to serve such a Lord.

Have *you* ever surrendered your hearts? Christ will not accept an unwilling gift, he does not ask your heart, unless you give it wholly, freely; but if you are willing to do that, *he* is both able and willing to save you. Are you united to Christ? Many among you have not even got the length of the foolish virgins; many of you have got no lamps at all; but to you who are carrying your lamps we speak, and we again simply ask, Are you, or are you not, united to Jesus? It is no light matter. It is not the unimportant trifle which some seem to consider it, whether or not you can answer this question. Oh! that you would even now begin, in the light of the Holy Ghost, to think on these things, to consider your latter end.

'They that were foolish took their lamps, and took no oil with them, but the wise took oil in their vessels with their lamps.' We are not told that any difference appeared between the foolish and the wise virgins; it is not even unlikely that, at the beginning, some of the lamps of the foolish virgins burned the brightest. Christians are judged of very differently by God from what man sees in them. Grace often dwells in the heart of some poor, despised, heart-broken one, who trembles at God's Word, and who is oppressed with doubt, fear, unbelief, and temptation, never hoping that he is a subject of grace; while many a flaming profession has nothing in it on which the eye of God can bear to look. We are thankful when we see a lamp burning brightly for one year, but how many of those that have been lighted are blown out. At Kilsyth, for instance, there are a few who, for some months, promised fair for heaven, but the light is extinguished. It reminds us of a nursery of young plants. The first year, when they are all lying close together in the plantation, they seem to thrive, and they are allowed to grow up together; but the second year they must be thinned, and only the choice plants can be given a place in the ground; in successive years they are thinned, and thinned again, and what a small, small number of the original seedlings remain in the dark forest of a hundred years. It is just so, in the spiritual world, especially when there has been a great awakening. At first, there are numbers of professors, the crowd follows Jesus. There is no shame, no reproach, and it is easy to follow him when there is no cross on the way. But in a short time, when religion is no longer the fashion of the day, when the crowd forsakes him, then too many of those whose lamps for a time seemed to burn the brightest, turn back, and walk no more with Jesus.

Some go further than this, their lamps remain lighted for a longer time, and while all goes on smoothly, and they remain in the society of their Christian friends, they find that, after all, it is rather a comfortable thing to serve God; but when they have to sacrifice something that is peculiarly dear to them, or else to give up Christ, it is found that they have been hypocrites all along. Friends, what madness, not to give up everything gladly, freely, for Christ! Remember, I beseech you, these affecting words of the Lord, 'What shall it profit a man, if he shall gain the whole world, and lose his own soul?' None can tell in this world, how many, once promising professors, have been ruined by the example and influence of the ungodly. I daresay those of you who are old enough, remember examples of this at Moulin. One man married an ungodly wife, and that cost him his soul; some woman married an ungodly husband, and that cost her her soul. Some fell in the time of reproach on account of the Word, and alas! too many, have continued in the sunshine of worldly property so long, that the riches of this world and the cares of this life, have sprung up and choked the Word.

O, prosperity! prosperity! who can resist thy baneful influences? Who ever stood thy unclouded sunshine? Who ever escaped unhurt from thine unceasing smile? There is nothing, nothing so difficult as to escape this; indeed, we may say at once, that without a great degree of the influence of the Spirit of God, it is impossible. Blessed be Jehovah's name, that with him all things, the very greatest of human impossibilities, are possible. Commonly speaking, however, this is not the case; it too often happens, and I think it is perhaps just the greatest proof of the fearful depravity of our nature, that all God's gifts are, one after another, turned in measure against the Giver.

Sometimes the lamp of profession will last even for a longer period, and the lamp burns on with its deceitful flame, even till that solemn hour when it lights the sinner to the entrance of the dark valley. It leaves him there *alone*. It is a fearful discovery to make at such an hour as that, that a man has been walking in the directly opposite road from heaven all his life, and walking in it at ease; that he has been carrying all his life a lamp which, in the hour of need, is to leave him in the dark.

We are not left in ignorance as to the cause of this, it is contained in the verses 3 and 4 of this chapter. 'They that were foolish took their lamps, and took no oil with them. But the wise took oil in their vessels with their lamps.' Here is the secret of the difference. The foolish virgins' lamps may not only burn on till a dying hour, they may go further still (for the wicked have often no bands in their death); the lamp may lead them fearless to the judgment-seat, nor go out till they reach the bar of God. They have got no oil with them. They have got light enough to maintain a consistent outward profession, but they have never got Christ, they have never got the Spirit of Christ; they have no secret supplies in themselves, and they have got no key to the treasure-house.

Believer, you feel that in yourself you have no good thing, no supply of grace, no faith, no light, no love; but then the more you are conscious of that, the more will you confide in that everlasting provision, that exhaustless fountain that sends forth the rich streams of heavenly blessing to poor dead souls: even in that Holy Spirit who is come into the world to convince it of sin, of righteousness, and of judgment, and to take of the things of Christ and shew them to men's souls. Though you have been savingly and abidingly united to Christ, you still need to come afresh every hour, just as for the first time.

The provision we receive at once is sometimes great, but it soon needs renewing. When you have gone to rest at night, after getting very near to God in prayer, feeling that you had certainly got enough to last till the morning, yet when morning came, with its vanities and its cares, you felt the need of carrying back your empty vessel to the fountain of living water to get it replenished. Sweet to lay down an empty soul at the feet of a Saviour, who filleth all in all! Take care to have your lamps always trimmed, for-listen—'While the bridegroom tarried they all slumbered and slept.' I do not mean to say that the lamp which has once been lighted by the Spirit can ever go out. It cannot, it will not. But beware, beware, that you have indeed received the grace of Christ, that you have indeed seen his glory. Have oil in your vessels with your lamps. The coming of the bridegroom is here shewn to be an unexpected event. We should all be on our guard; he will not come when he is expected. Watch and pray, lest, coming suddenly, he find you sleeping. It is a sad surprise to a Christian when he is not ready for his Master's coming; it is a sad surprise to find himself unprepared, his books all unsummed up, even though he may have been a faithful servant. This is the chief object of desire which he has presented to his dear people. Whenever the people of God have been in a lively frame, ever since his ascension, their desire for his second coming has always been the greater. His last words to the church are, 'I come quickly.' Now, are you all adding your Amen; or are some of you secretly wishing that it might be just a little longer deferred, and then you would have made up your mind to part with all that is now so dear to you, and then you would be ready and willing to go with Jesus home to heaven. But, friends, if you feel thus towards Christ's second coming, unless you are hasting unto it, examine, examine, I beseech you, e'er it be too late, and do not rest until you discover if your profession be really genuine. Better, if need be, make the mournful discovery on this side death, than to find out only at the judgment-seat that you have been self-deceived hypocrites. It is said that the coming of Jesus will be as a thief in the night. It will be in the dark. Though in a far more fearful sense he will come in the night to the foolish virgins to cast them into outer darkness, this is also true of his coming to believers.

It will be without a warning. You know that it is generally prefaced by some bodily distress or affliction, as it were, to prepare for the last scene, and the more you are enabled to be in such a state of preparation, the more likely will your death be either peaceful or triumphant. In whatever state of solemn preparation you may be, it will be a sudden and overawing surprise to a soul, to find that it has crossed the Jordan of death, and floated away out of the stream of time, to see the King in his beauty.

Every figure used to represent this to us brings the suddenness of it to mind, but none so much as that of a thief in the night. A thief never comes in the day time, he does not like the sunshine, it does not suit him; he won't come when the moon is shining brightly, for then he might be detected, and easily found out. No, no, the thief does not like the moonshine, he would not like even a very starry night, but he likes a dark, cloudy, evening, when the shades are deep. He comes at midnight when it is pitch dark, and when all men are asleep. Now, believers, this is the way he will come to you, and he tells you this, so that you may be watching and ready, for you see his followers are sometimes slumbering and sleeping, when the cry is heard—'Behold the bridegroom cometh!' Oh! for a well-trimmed lamp. Oh! that you would, every one of you, see that your lamps are all burning, that they are all trimmed, and that besides you have oil in your vessels with your lamps. Are you not afraid, you that think yourselves Christians, that your lamps at last will go out? The words, 'Ye must be born again,' ring in our ears. Unless you are sure that that great change of conversion has passed in your soul, don't you think you have reason to tremble? You do not know but your lamps may go out. I do not know whether my lamp may not go out.

Does it not make you tremble to see the lamp of Judas shine so long? Does it not make you cry out, 'Lord, is it I? Lord is it I?' Better, far better, ask with all the apostles that awful question now, than read the fearful answer for the first time in hell. And, remember too, that not only those who shall be saved, now ask that question with anxious fear, for Judas too asked, 'Lord, is it I?' Men and brethren, be up and doing; 'strait is the gate, and narrow is the way' are words that seem almost forgotten in these days of ease, carelessness, and sin. They are not expunged from the Bible. No, the gate is as strait, the way is as narrow as it was on the day that Jesus proclaimed to disbelieving Jerusalem, that few there be that go in thereat. It reminds us of the gate which you find at the toll-bar, when, during the night, the wide gate is locked. You know there is always a small turn-stile at the one side of the wide road, contrived in such a way that nothing larger than a man can pass through it. Neither can more than one man pass at a time, each one must go alone. This is using a familiar illustration, which you must all understand. It is just so with the narrow gate to heaven. All men are going along the same road,—the broad road of life—leading its millions down to eternal death. Now the wide gate stands open all day long, and there is always a crowd passing through it. The broad road is just the road in which the poor, blind sinners are born, brought up, and carried along by the thoughtless crowd. It is the way they have always walked in; it is the road their fathers passed over; it is the way which they see thronged by their relations, companions, neighbours, friends; and it is a road they never think of leaving. By the side of the wide gate stands the narrow gate of life, heaven, and glory; and Jesus stands upon that narrow path, and calls to all the poor, weary travellers to ruin, to come to him, and he will give them rest. He tells them he is able, he tells them he is willing. he tells them he is near, to help and save them, and stretches forth his hands, all the day, to a disobedient and gain-saying people. A chosen few, drawn by his resistless grace, he brings to himself, and he will lead them till he carries them on to glory.

Sometimes the crowd is so mixed, that those who pass along mistake which road they tread. But, however closely the two ways may run together, they end as widely apart as heaven and hell. Every man, woman, and child among you is walking along either the one or the other of these ways. The one ends in life eternal, the other in death. Which are you in? Which are you in? Eternal life! Eternal death! Which is yours?

Are we to go away to-night without a blessing, without one soul for Jesus? Oh, that the former days of Moulin were revived with tenfold power! Oh, that the Spirit, who, not forty years ago, was poured out in Moulin—in this very place, on the same ground on which we stand—were to be poured out in rich abundance, that the dry, parched wilderness might rejoice and blossom as the rose. Christians, will you not pray for Moulin, that it may again become a very garden of the Lord.

Brothers, sisters, are you going to choose destruction, are you going to stand out against the entreaties of Immanuel, the strivings of the Spirit? You hear how all around you, people are coming into Christ. Blessed be God, the question is already asked, 'Who are these that fly as a cloud, and as the doves to their windows?' The poor world is already beginning to stagger at the unaccountable change that has come over some who used to be just as sensible, firm, and manly, as they. I doubt not that there is sometimes a strange sinking of heart as they pronounce them silly, mad, woman-hearted, an involuntary asking, 'How am I to account for this in such a one? What has made these calm, reasoning, quiet, respectable men, these good neighbours, that have always been as regular in their duties, as sober and as kind to their families, and as punctual in their performance of every duty as I am, begin to say so much about new hearts?' It is so incomprehensible to them, and yet so powerful, so brightly glorious in its effects, that they are filled with wonder. Is the same question, 'Who are these that fly as the doves to their windows?' not to be asked of Moulin? There have been many coming to Christ in Scotland. Only weak women? Nay, I have seen strong, sturdy men, in the very pride of youth, of manhood, and of sin, bend till they nearly sank. So near yourselves as Aberfeldy, I saw it only last Friday, when there was a marvellous impression made, as some present well know, which, God grant, may be followed up by a work of conversion, if these impressions do not dissipate again. Yes, men of Kilsyth have come to Christ, men of Dundee, men of Perth; there is a little band of new disciples in Kilsyth, in Dundee, in Perth, is there not to be one in Moulin? Are we not to get you for Christ, sons of the mountains?

We long to see the prayers of the saints that lie in yon churchyard answered. They float in the heaven over your heads like clouds of blessing, clouds that were attracted to heaven by the rays of the Sun of Righteousness. Forty years ago, His rays sped down, and poured light, and heat, and glory over this fair land, that had long been dwelling in spiritual darkness. We long to see the clouds which are bending towards your mountain tops, called for as they are by a parched soil, called for also now by the prayers of children's children. Your fathers made Moulin in their day like a city set upon an hill, which could not be hid. Coming towards this place, I overtook a middle-aged labourer on the road, and when he was asked one or two questions about his spiritual state, he seemed quite astonished. When he was asked whether he was a Christian, he looked with unfeigned amazement in the face of the speaker, and said, 'A Christian! Oh, sir, we're all Christians here; why do you ask that?' Poor man! I daresay there were many such Christians as he in the place where he lived.

Are there none here of whom Jesus said, 'I pray for them,' none that are to look back on this night, and say, 'On that Sabbath evening the Spirit awoke me from sleep. On that Sabbath evening I first saw Christ. It was then my bleeding conscience found peace in the blood of the Lamb?'

Sinner, open your heart to Jesus. You would not keep the Queen waiting for admission, or even your landlord. There never was such a thing heard of, as to keep a landlord waiting! You never even kept a friend, a relation, a neighbour, perhaps some of you never kept a poor beggar waiting at your door. And yet you, who have not yet freely embraced Christ, you have been keeping the glorious Immanuel, the blessed and only potentate, King of kings, and Lord of lords, waiting, and waiting, and waiting, at the door of your poor, dark, blinded hearts. Yes, the King of kings, by whom princes reign, has knocked, and knocked and knocked repeatedly, again and again, and the door is still shut. To-night, he still is standing at the door. Is he to see the portals of one heart, the everlasting doors of one hitherto barred dungeon, lift up their heads to let the King of Glory enter in? You have an open door to sin, to folly, an open door to the devil; and yet, it is shut against Jesus, against God, against the Spirit. 'Behold, I stand at the door and knock; if any man hear my voice, and open the door, I will come in to him and will sup with him, and he with me.' Will you not say, 'Welcome, Immanuel, as all my salvation'?

16

SIN CONDEMNED

[*Preached to the congregation of the Rev. Dr C. J. Brown, Free New North, Edinburgh, while they worshipped in the Potterrow, December 1846. Burns had just returned from Canada. The claims of China, in connection with the resolution of the English Presbyterian Church to start a mission in that great empire, were strongly pressed upon him. The result was his giving himself to that service, and being ordained at Sunderland on 22d April 1847.*]

'FOR WHAT THE LAW COULD NOT DO, IN THAT IT WAS WEAK THROUGH THE FLESH, GOD SENDING HIS OWN SON IN THE LIKENESS OF SINFUL FLESH, AND FOR SIN, CONDEMNED SIN IN THE FLESH.'—*Romans 8. 3.*

The word 'flesh' in this verse seems to stand for the nature of fallen man, and shortly expresses what we might, in other words, call, man's nature forsaken by God's Spirit. The Lord Jehovah having left the place designed for him in the human heart, his place is taken by another. Sin has its seat in the flesh. It reigns there unopposed in the natural man. It has many and varied manifestations; on these we cannot enter, they are innumerable. They are as many as the man has faculties, and, in short, in all the ways in which man is now capable of thinking and acting, he is sinning. The word 'flesh,' then, as here used, does not refer to the body, but rather to man's whole nature, destitute of the Spirit of God.

This gives us a very deep view of sin, and shews us how firmly it is entrenched, and how securely lodged in the heart; and there is no form in which it appears so much to be sin, or so utterly vile and hideous, as that spoken of in the seventh verse, where it is said that 'the carnal mind is enmity against God.' There are indeed some aspects in which sin is more easily detected, but here is a form of it which prevails universally in all who have not been made free in Christ Jesus. What an opening up is this of the state of man's mind! 'It is not subject to the law of God, neither indeed can be.' It can submit to no control, to no government, however just, and wise, and good, but must of necessity continue to rebel and to widen hourly the breach between the soul and the Lord God who made it, thus rendering it an impossibility that any natural man should, at any moment, or by any act, please God. 'They that are in the flesh cannot please God.' Ah, my dear friends, if our eyes were opened, this would indeed seem a fearful statement, and one calculated to shut up every sinner present to the faith of the Son of God.

But let us now consider the means which *cannot* deliver from this awful state. The law of God, the statute-law of the kingdom, written by the Lord himself—unerring, perfect, holy, divine—of this law it is said, 'What the law could not do.' To what is it then declared impotent? To condemn sin in the flesh. True, in one sense it does this; the tables of the old covenant were written for this. The law discovers sin, forbids it, passes sentence upon it, threatens eternal death upon the commission of it, pronouncing a fearful curse upon the smallest violation of the commandment, and in this way sin is condemned; but the impotence of the law lies in this, that it cannot condemn sin with power to destroy; it *can* condemn the sinner to death, and it can hold him fast, so that no creature may deliver; and it can carry out the sentence by destroying him, and causing him to suffer for ever, in the name, and by the authority of God, whose minister it is. But this is all the law can do; and, ah, brethren, there is little hope for a poor sinner here. The law cannot help him against his sins, it cannot even drive the love of them from his bosom; and though it brings sin to the light, and exposes it there to all the commands, and the curses, and the threatenings with which the law is armed, instead of dying, *sin revives*. This is what is meant by these words, 'the law entered that the offence might abound.'

Paul tells us something of a sinner's experience when this holy law comes in contact with him and his iniquities,— 'For I was alive without the law once, but when the commandment came, sin revived and I died;' not *sin died*, but *I died*. There is a great difference between the sinner being condemned, and sin being condemned. Ah! there is no view of sin that shews its dreadful Satanic power more than this, or that proves the difficulty of rooting it out of the heart more than this, that even God's holy law cannot do it. A law, holy, just, and good, approving itself to the sinner's conscience, armed with awful sanctions, holding in its hand life and death eternal, speaking with the voice and authority of Jehovah. What could be stronger? What more likely to influence and be obeyed by intelligent creatures? And yet, when this law comes into direct contact with sin, it is found to be 'weak through the flesh.' There is something in sin that turns aside the weapon, something so stupifying that every warning is of no avail.

Oh, fellow-sinner, are you awake to this? Do you know that your heart is so ungodly, so desperately bad, that it makes the most perfect instrument that God can use or devise ineffectual? Oh, it might terrify men out of their sleep, to hear that they are yielding complacently to the dominion of that which is so vile, so polluting, and yet so strong, that it can neither be transformed nor subdued, nor extinguished by any of the workings of the holy and mighty government of God. What an awful thing to be a servant of that which can only be put a stop to by shutting it up in hell for ever to die the second death! Surely, then, this view of sin might teach you many lessons of your own helplessness. Men think that sin will bow to *them!* and that *they* can tame it down by reformations, and good resolutions, and efforts of their own! It does not bow to the very law of God; so that at Mount Sinai, when just given, and before Moses had time to bring it down to them, the poor Israelites set about making a golden calf.

And now let us inquire, how it is that the law has no strength to condemn sin. The first reason is, that it can provide no *remission* for sin. It comes seeking obedience, and when it finds not that, it goes no further, it pronounces a curse. It is this that makes it so worthy of God; it never makes a compromise, nor lowers its demands, and yet all the while pursues the sinner for payment, his conscience being on the side of the law, and witness against himself. You see, then, that unless a way could be found in which sin could be remitted, man must continue to flee farther and farther from God, and to increase in enmity to him. But, secondly, the law is weak in respect to this, that it possesses no *sanctifying power*; although it *commands* obedience, it provides no gracious power to *create* obedience. The law was suited to man in a state of holiness, but it can have nothing to do with any works that are not perfect, it turns away from all such. If only men knew and realized this, how differently would they listen to the gospel! In most people's experience, I believe, the gospel is virtually regarded as unnecessary; spoken about, it is true, but merely spoken about, because there is so much of it in the Bible, and not from any deep heartfelt need of it in the sinner's bosom. This arises from their ignorance of the law; they do not believe in its stern, uncompromising character; they do not believe that it gives no help to an awakened sinner, and that no provision is in it to enable him to return to God. Viewed at a distance, the law looks as if it might destroy sin, but when it comes near, and shows the sinner a true picture of himself, sin rises and rebels, and becomes exceeding sinful indeed; every convinced soul is brought to acknowledge this, and to say that the law is 'weak through the flesh,' and can do nothing to bring him nigh to God.

Let us now contemplate for a little *the means which do accomplish* the final destruction of sin. It would seem that none could be more mighty than the law, which holds death and life, blessing and curse, in its righteous hand; but the Lord appears, and the simple, glorious means is this, that God sent his own Son. This is the beginning of a sinner's hope. *God sent his own Son!* What an awful thing is sin proved to be—how fearful its power—how wondrous the work of condemning it, when Jehovah took a way to do it so altogether without example or parallel in the universe; *not* by the curse of the law, *not* by any works on man's part, but by his own Son, sent in the reality of human nature, but only in the likeness of sinful flesh and of fallen man. Mystery of love! Great without controversy! and yet this is the only means sufficiently powerful to condemn sin.

Do you ask how this intervention of the Son of God condemns sin? By exposing its vile, unalterable, malignant nature, when it can neither be weakened, condemned, nor destroyed, but by so unheard-of a means as this, even the sending forth of Immanuel in the likeness of the rebellious creature, to be marred, and bruised, and slain in his room. Surely sin is condemned thus, and sentence passed on it as evil, when heaven must give up the only begotten Son, before it can be destroyed. Think of this.

Not only does the sending forth of God's Son shew in a clearer light than the law can do, that sin is an evil and bitter thing; it passes a sentence of death on it, and slays it by satisfying the law: 'The strength of sin is the law.' We think by nature that the law is the death of sin, whereas the law is so much the strength of sin, that it not only provides no sanctifying power in itself for the sinner, but it stands by, as it were, to see that he gets no relief from any other quarter. The very grace of God cannot reach him, because of this offended, dishonoured law. Even had the Lord—to speak with reverence—desired to give man his Holy Spirit, he could not give any of his glorious blessings to one lying under the sentence of death, for the law stands in the way.

Suppose a destroying serpent were in your house, and you took a sword to slay it, but a beloved child was in the way between the serpent and you, so that you could not strike the one, without piercing the other, you dare not destroy the object of your love in order to slay the reptile. Thus the Lord cannot give his Holy Spirit to subdue your sins, without first satisfying the law; *that* were to give life at the expense of his own holiness; and so the law stands at the sinner's side, crying, 'Pay me that thou owest!' But oh! when the Son of God came down, and appeared to take the sinner's place, there was no longer any obstacle to God's giving the Spirit to destroy sin in his heart. The evil of sin was held up, and the law, which is its strength, was taken out of the way, while the gift of the Spirit was provided for the sanctification of the very vilest. He endured the curse of a broken covenant, and then the way was opened for the descending Spirit.

A way opened! Oh how wondrous is this new and living way! The lost sinner beholds it, and begins to commit himself, soul, body, and spirit, to Jesus, and to rest his hope of a free, full, final pardon, not on anything he can ever do, but on the Surety of the covenant; and then the Spirit of Jehovah comes freely forth to glorify Jesus and renew the heart, and to nail sin to the cross, not dead, but under sentence; and every time the Spirit puts himself forth in the believer's soul, is a fresh intimation given to sin of coming death; and then the law is loved, and gloriously set up in the soul; and now it is that the believer, who flies to Christ, and finds that there is no condemnation, can testify that the law of the Spirit of life in Christ Jesus hath made him free from the law of sin and death. True, there is a constant fight; but then he will be more than conqueror soon, and meanwhile he walks after the Spirit, he makes deliberate choice of all that the Spirit suggests; and though the flesh trouble him, it is not he that is running after the flesh, but the flesh that is walking after him; it will continue to oppress and pursue him, so that he is ever crying for deliverance, but he will be freed from its very presence when he is gone to be present with Immanuel.

And now, what should the unconverted learn from all this? The unconverted—who are they? how may they be known? They are those who are 'after the flesh,' and unlike the believer, who flees from sin, and escapes as for his life, they walk after it, and seek its gratification all the day long in some form or other. True, you will not allow this; you consider yourselves above yielding to the lusts of the flesh; you do not like to hear men thus divided into two classes; you would rather not be troubled with hearing so much about conversion and a new heart. But, oh! brethren, the line would need to be put very plainly down in these days, when men do not know their own faces in the glass of God's Word. You are running on in sin with the world, pursuing it, devouring it, though God is warning you, and sounding his awful threatenings in your ears. If this be true of you, you are not converted; your own consciences tell you so. The man who is walking after the Spirit does the opposite from this. Hating the body of death which drags him down, and mourning when he is overtaken by it, he groans for relief, longing after God, crying for grace, seeking the extermination of sin. Who among *you* are doing this? Who among *you* are resisting sin unto the death? *As many only in this house* as are led by the Spirit *now!* Ah! dear fellow-sinner, sin is no trifle. Its guilt is no trifle. Its power is such, that none but the Spirit of Jehovah can kill it, and emancipate the soul. Your resolutions will not do this, friends cannot do it for you, your own will cannot do it, knowledge cannot do it; and your refuge is, therefore, in the crucified Lamb! There is no other refuge—none! Yet, don't be deceived here, fellow-sinners! Some think they are hidden there, who are only sleeping on a notion about grace and the blood of Jesus. They are cleaving to the covenant by flatteries, and there is too much of that in these professing days. Oh! but is there in this house a poor sinner, lying burdened and groaning, under the load and power of sin? Look, then, here! Lift up your eyes, and see what a provision! Look to that great, glorious Redeemer! Hear him! What is he saying? '*Come unto me.*' And you will come, you will value him, and you shall find salvation.

All God's people know what it is to be convinced of sin, and to flee to the hiding-place; but I would ask you, believers, is this your *present experience?* If you are not realising it, go to Jesus now; go as for the first time. Ah! do not go back to walk after the flesh. Are you resting in the warfare? Are you looking with more toleration upon sin, and with less alarm upon that vile, God-dishonouring unbelief that makes you doubt his word? are you fainting, beloved, and saying you need rest? Ah! but this is not your rest. This is the time for pursuing the enemy, and for disputing every inch of ground with Satan, for wrestling, and fighting, and watching, and it will be so to the end; and your rest will come yet, a long, long, eternal Sabbath rest above. Oh, is there any soul here who is becoming *slothful?* I fear there are many, many such, many who are lazy and idle in fighting against sin. 'Be not slothful,' up and be doing; the day is coming when the battle will end, and you shall have rest. Sin is yet to be destroyed. It is now a criminal in confinement, waiting for execution. The hour of final victory is nigh at hand; and when it comes, there will be no wandering thought, no vile affection, no body of death.

And what does all this teach us with regard to contributing for Christ's cause on the earth?—how does it bear on the object of this day's collection for raising means to send the gospel to the poor heathen in distant lands and dark corners of the earth? You know well, that 'without holiness no man shall see the Lord;' so that it is utterly impossible for one single soul among these perishing millions to enter glory. If it were possible, the law must leave heaven when such an one entered; or rather, brethren, it would follow the sinner into heaven, and pluck him from the very presence of Jehovah, down to the pit of destruction. And if this be true of every man in a Christian land, of the most amiable, virtuous, generous man, who knows not gospel holiness, what is to become of the heathen? Who ever heard of a holy heathen? True, the men of the world are pleased with many of them, and would almost rather see them remain heathens still. But ah! the servants of Christ feel very differently; and you who are believers belie your profession, if you would not give all you had, yea, and your own selves also, if others were not ready to aid, and to carry forth the gospel among them. Look abroad; look not at tens of thousands merely in this land, but look yonder and see millions, millions perishing, rushing on, in darkness, down to the pit.

A LETTER TO THE PEOPLE IN THE HIGHLANDS OF PERTHSHIRE

[*The affection with which Mr Burns was regarded, wherever he went, by those who attended his ministry, was doubly manifested towards him by the ardent Highlanders. From the Highland districts which he visited, as from his other scenes of labour, he received so many letters of gratitude and of inquiry, that it was impossible for him to reply to them. He would sometimes write a letter to be read by the ministers to the people, who would at once have it printed, that each might possess a copy. His last visit to the Highlands was paid in the year 1854, when, having returned from China for a few months, he went north from Perth by Blair-Atholl and Tummel Bridge in the first week of December. He reminded his hearers of his deep regret, while among them formerly, that he could not address them in the Gaelic tongue; but said he could now at least read to them a chapter in it, having learned as much in Canada from the Highlanders there.*]

MY DEAR FRIENDS,

I have often thought of writing to you, but have been hitherto prevented by various causes; and I now take up my pen in great haste to send you a few hurried lines, praying that Jehovah, the God of all grace, may enable me to say a word in season to each of your precious and dearly beloved souls.

It has given me unfeigned joy to hear that those appearances of spiritual concern, which I was privileged of

God to witness among you, have *not* proved in every case as the morning cloud, and as the early dew; but that some among you who seemed, when I was among you, to be entering in at the strait gate, are still following on to know the Lord. It is a sweet and sure consolation to me to think that the work is Jehovah's, and his alone; that he *will* have mercy on whom he will have mercy; and that, though many, alas! may, and actually do, abuse their privileges, and grieve away the Holy Ghost, and are left, in righteous judgment, to follow their own ways and perish, yet the Lord *will* pluck his own chosen ones as brands from the burning, and will put his fear in their hearts, so that they *shall not* depart from him.

1. Blessed indeed are *those among you whom God has called by his grace to the fellowship of his Son.* Your blessedness, believers in Jesus, is infinitely greater than the tongue of archangel can express. *Now* are we the sons of God; and it doth not yet appear what we shall be; but we know that when he shall appear we shall be like him, for we shall see him as he is. All things are yours, whether Paul, or Apollos, or Cephas, or the world, or life, or death, all are yours; and ye are Christ's, and Christ is God's! True it is, my dear brethren in the Lord, that you must, through much tribulation, enter the Kingdom. All that will live godly in Christ Jesus shall suffer persecution. You will be hated by an unrighteous and ungodly world; assaulted and buffeted by a cunning and malicious devil; and, above all, deceived, and in danger of being destroyed by a desperately wicked heart. But be encouraged, fainting believer, he that shall come will come, and will not tarry. Then shall the battle be over, the victory be gained, the crown of glory be bestowed by the hand of Jesus! Then we shall see face to

face that adorable and matchless One whom, not having seen, we love. Then shall we join the blood-washed throng in crying, 'Worthy is the Lamb that was slain, who hath redeemed us to God with his blood, and hath made us kings and priests to God and the Father', and we shall 'reign for ever and ever!'

How sweet the trials of a Christian are when he meets with Jesus in them, and feels that the Lord is making them a means of purging away his dross, and taking away all his sin. The believer's trials are like the fiery furnace to the three children of Israel at Babylon, which burned off their bands, but touched not a hair of their heads. Seek, dear followers of the despised Immanuel, to obtain glimpses of his divine glory and grace, through the power of the indwelling Spirit, and these will make you to see such a surpassing beauty and glory in Jesus, that you will count all things loss that you may win him, and be found in him. If you find the way to glory hard and rugged, oh! think what it cost the Son of God to open up that way! Remember also that, wherever you are called to go, in following the Lamb, you may see, by faith, the prints of Immanuel's feet on the path before you. He *does* lead his people through fire and through water, but it is to *a wealthy place*. Soon will he come to call us home to the place prepared for us above. Soon he will offer up for us the prayer, 'Father, I will that they whom thou hast given me be with me where I am, that they may behold my glory,' and then shall we depart and be with Jesus! To them that look for him, he will appear the second time without sin unto salvation! Now the just shall live by faith; but, if any man draw back, my soul, saith God, shall have no pleasure in him. May none of you be of them that draw back unto perdition; may you all be of those who believe unto the saving of the soul.

Let me exhort you, beloved, with a view to your perseverance in the good ways of the Lord, to feed continually upon Jesus Christ and him crucified, as he is made known in the holy Word of God, and by the Holy Ghost. For this purpose read the Bible much, and pray continually over it for the saving illumination of the Spirit. Examine your hearts frequently in regard to your acquaintance with sin, and your knowledge of the Lord Jesus. See that you be wholly dedicated to God in Christ; that his holy, heart-searching law be written on your hearts; and that you be aiming habitually with a single eye at the advancement of the divine glory. It was the common saying of an eminent saint (Brainerd), that nothing else made him content to remain in this world for a single day, but that God could be seen and could be served in it. This is the language of the heart of every true saint; though, alas! few can say it with such emphasis as he.

Let me press upon you, also, to make the truly godly your only companions, and to seek that God may greatly bless to you the fellowship of the saints. Avoid, I beseech you, in all things the very *appearance* of evil; and make it manifest, by your holy, pure, humble, meek, spiritual, and consistent walk, that you are no more of the world, but have been born of God, and are preparing to enter into the holy kingdom of your Father who is in heaven. Finally, let me exhort you to keep the conscience always clean and peaceful, by beholding the bleeding Lamb of God as your Surety and Saviour, to put on the divine righteousness of Jesus as the only covering of the guilty, naked soul, at the bar of divine justice, and to be filled with the Holy Ghost, who quickens, sanctifies, comforts, supports, and at last glorifies the soul in which he dwells!

2. But what shall I say to *those among you who have neither part nor lot in the matter of salvation?* Alas! your case, dear fellow-sinners, is awful indeed, little as it now affects your own blinded souls. My heart is ready to break for you, when I think that, after all the solemn warnings you have received, and after all the pressing offers of Jesus that have been made to you in the name of God, you still remain in a state of heart-ungodliness, or of open sin! Others around you can this day say with joy, 'Now is our salvation nearer than when we believed:' but of you it is written in the Word of the holy and unchangeable God: 'Their judgment now of a long time lingereth not, and their damnation slumbereth not!' Oh! dear fellow-sinner, is it not the height of madness to go on any longer in a Christless state? You know well that except a man be born again he cannot see the kingdom of God; that the time is at hand when the Lord Jesus will appear in the clouds of heaven, with his mighty angels, taking vengeance on all that know not God and that obey not the gospel of our Lord Jesus Christ, and that these shall be punished with everlasting destruction from the presence of the Lord and the glory of his power! You *may* go on a *little* longer without being cast into hell; but oh, how *soon* will death, the king of terrors, come and drag you to the bar of God! You *may* avoid the Throne of Grace, but you *cannot* escape the Throne of Judgment! You *may* despise Jesus as a Saviour; you *cannot* but tremble before him as a Judge! You *may* reject him as the Lamb of God; but, alas, you *must* endure his consuming wrath as the Lion of the tribe of Judah! You *will* not weep for sin *now*, but you *must* weep

for it *hereafter*! You *shall* mourn for sin in hell, if you do not mourn for it on earth! Ah! tell me why you reject the Lord? What fault can you find in Jesus? Have you found any other Saviour? Oh! dear fellow-sinner, it is high time for you to awake out of sleep!

Arise and come to Jesus *now*. He is crying, Come unto me, I will in no wise cast you out. The Father is ready to receive you into his family. The Spirit is striving with you, did you not resist him and grieve him away. Halt no longer between two opinions. Sin and Satan are ruining you; knowledge cannot save you, decency cannot save you, profession cannot save you, conviction cannot save you; you may go to hell with the arrows of the Almighty festering in the conscience; nothing will avail but the blood and the Spirit of Jesus. Yield yourself, then, to the Lord as a lost sinner, and he will not cast you out. You have seen individuals around you, perhaps some of your own friends or companions, fleeing to Jesus; why did you not follow them? Are you resolved to be left behind in Sodom and to perish in the flames!

Do I seem to you, dear fellow-sinner, as one that mocks, when I thus warn you. Ah! remember it was so in the days of Noah. The old world thought him, no doubt, a self-righteous fool, when he warned them that the world was about to be devoured by the floods of God's vengeance; but they saw that he was divinely wise, when he entered into the ark and the flood came and destroyed them all! Soon will the deluge of everlasting wrath roll over this guilty, sin-stained earth, and sweep away, in its devouring, relentless waves, the whole world of the ungodly! Then will the penitent followers of Jesus rest secure upon the Rock of Ages, and look down without fear upon the horrific floods below! Ah, sinner! what joy will the pleasures of sin give you *then?* will you laugh, and dance, and drink with your companions *then?* Ah, no, you will rue the day that you were born! you will curse the day that you heard the gospel and despised the Saviour! Yea, you will even hear the words that I am now writing to you ringing in your ears, and adding new anguish to your unutterable torment! Do not, I beseech you, leave the place where you now are until you have given yourself up to the Lord, who still waiteth to be gracious. Will you yet delay? Oh! it is the suggestion of Satan, your murderer; yield at last to the love of God, put the crown upon Immanuel, save your soul, disappoint the devil, and give the angels a song of joy in heaven. May the Holy Ghost descend in his almighty power and prevail with you. May you *now* escape from that miserable company, the unregenerate, against whom the Lord's messengers, and I among the rest, must stand as witnesses at the judgment-seat of Christ, to condemn them to the second death.

Unworthy as these lines are of appearing in print, they will at least serve to put many of you in mind of those glorious days of the power and grace of the God which we enjoyed together last autumn, days which we shall all remember, either with grief or joy, throughout an endless eternity. Oh, that these days were now to return among you with tenfold greater glory, and that multitudes who have hitherto withstood every call of God that has been made to them by their own ministers and by strangers, were at last persuaded to repent and turn to God through Jesus Christ! Oh, that the Holy Ghost were now poured out upon many thousands among you in his convincing, converting, sanctifying, and comforting power! Plead, dear fellow-sinners, for this infinite promise of the Father, which we have heard of Jesus. Ye that make mention of the Lord, keep not silence, and *give him no rest*, until he arise and make Jerusalem a praise among you, and throughout the whole earth.

Commending you all to the infinite, free, sovereign, and everlasting grace of Jehovah, and desiring an interest in the prayers of the Lord's children among you,

I remain, Your affectionate and humble servant in the Lord,

WM. C. BURNS.

GRANDTULLY, *June 11, 1841.*